Mobile Identity Management

James Relington

DEDICATION

This book is dedicated to all the professionals working tirelessly to secure digital identities and protect organizations from ever-evolving threats. To the cybersecurity teams, IT administrators, and identity management experts who ensure safe and seamless access for users—your work is invaluable. And to my family and friends, whose support and encouragement made this journey possible, thank you.

AKNOWLEDGEMENTS

I would like to express my deepest gratitude to everyone who contributed to the creation of this book. To my colleagues and mentors in the cybersecurity and identity management field, your insights and expertise have been invaluable. To the organizations and professionals who shared their experiences and best practices, your contributions have enriched this work. A special thanks to my family and friends for their unwavering support and encouragement throughout this journey. Finally, to the readers, thank you for your interest in identity lifecycle management—may this book help you navigate the evolving landscape of digital security with confidence.

Introduction to Mobile Identity

In today's digital landscape, identity has become one of the most crucial aspects of online interactions. As mobile technology continues to evolve, mobile identity management has emerged as a critical component of securing and streamlining digital experiences. Mobile identity refers to the digital representation of an individual, device, or entity that enables authentication, authorization, and access control in mobile environments. With the increasing reliance on smartphones and other mobile devices for personal and professional activities, managing identities in these ecosystems has become both a necessity and a challenge.

The rise of mobile identity is closely linked to the rapid growth of mobile computing and cloud services. Users now expect seamless access to applications, services, and data from anywhere, often across multiple devices. This shift has led to the need for more sophisticated identity management solutions that can adapt to dynamic environments while ensuring security and usability. Unlike traditional identity management systems, which often rely on static credentials such as usernames and passwords, mobile identity leverages a range of authentication methods, including biometrics, multi-factor authentication (MFA), and device-based recognition.

One of the primary drivers of mobile identity adoption is the convenience it offers. Mobile devices are inherently personal, always connected, and equipped with various sensors and capabilities that can enhance authentication processes. Features like fingerprint scanning, facial recognition, and behavioral biometrics provide a seamless way to verify a user's identity without requiring cumbersome passwords. Additionally, mobile devices can act as identity tokens, enabling single sign-on (SSO) and federated identity solutions that reduce friction while enhancing security.

Security remains a fundamental concern in mobile identity management. As mobile devices become the primary gateway to sensitive data and online services, they also become attractive targets for cybercriminals. Phishing attacks, credential theft, and mobile malware are common threats that can compromise identities and lead to unauthorized access. To mitigate these risks, organizations and technology providers implement advanced security measures, such as risk-based authentication, device attestation, and continuous authentication, which analyze contextual factors like user behavior, location, and device health to determine the legitimacy of access requests.

Another key aspect of mobile identity is its role in enabling a seamless and interconnected digital ecosystem. With the proliferation of cloud services, Internet of Things (IoT) devices, and decentralized identity models, mobile identity plays a crucial role in ensuring secure and efficient interactions between users, applications, and systems. For instance, mobile identity can facilitate secure access to smart home devices, enable frictionless payments, and streamline enterprise authentication processes. The integration of mobile identity with identity and access management (IAM) frameworks ensures that users can move across different platforms and services without compromising security or usability.

Regulatory compliance and data privacy are also significant factors influencing mobile identity management. Governments and regulatory bodies worldwide have introduced stringent data protection laws, such as the General Data Protection Regulation (GDPR) and the California Consumer Privacy Act (CCPA), which mandate strict controls over personal data handling. Organizations must ensure that their mobile identity solutions comply with these regulations by implementing measures such as data encryption, user consent mechanisms, and transparent data usage policies. Privacy-preserving technologies, such as decentralized identity models and self-sovereign identity (SSI), are gaining traction as they give users greater control over their personal information while reducing reliance on centralized identity providers.

The future of mobile identity is shaped by ongoing advancements in technology and evolving user expectations. Artificial intelligence (AI) and machine learning (ML) are playing an increasingly important role in identity verification and fraud detection. AI-driven behavioral analytics can assess user patterns to detect anomalies and prevent identity theft in real time. Additionally, the adoption of blockchain and decentralized identity solutions is transforming traditional identity management by providing more secure and user-centric alternatives.

Despite the many advantages of mobile identity, challenges remain. Standardization across different platforms and ecosystems is a persistent issue, as various identity providers and authentication mechanisms must work together to provide seamless interoperability. Additionally, balancing security and user experience is an ongoing struggle. While stronger authentication measures enhance security, they can also introduce friction that negatively impacts usability. Striking the right balance requires continuous innovation and collaboration between technology providers, regulatory bodies, and industry stakeholders.

Mobile identity is becoming an indispensable part of modern digital life. As organizations and individuals continue to rely on mobile devices for critical transactions, communication, and access to services, the importance of robust and secure identity management cannot be overstated. The evolution of mobile identity will continue to be driven by technological innovation, regulatory requirements, and user demands for greater convenience and security. By embracing emerging trends and addressing key challenges, mobile identity can serve as a foundation for a more secure and user-friendly digital future.

Evolution of Digital Identity

The concept of identity has existed for centuries, traditionally verified through physical documents such as passports, birth certificates, and national identification cards. However, with the rise of the internet and digital transformation, identity has shifted from a physical concept to a virtual one. Digital identity now plays a critical role in modern life, enabling access to online services, financial transactions, communication platforms, and enterprise systems. As technology has evolved, so too has the way digital identities are managed, secured, and authenticated, shaping the way individuals and organizations interact in an increasingly connected world.

The earliest form of digital identity emerged with the advent of computer systems and networked environments. In the early days of computing, identity management was a simple process, usually involving a username and password combination. This method provided a basic level of security, but as online services expanded, the need for more robust identity verification mechanisms became apparent. The introduction of email accounts, e-commerce platforms, and online banking services led to an increase in identity-related security challenges, including password breaches and identity theft.

As internet usage became widespread in the late 1990s and early 2000s, digital identity systems evolved to address growing security concerns. The introduction of centralized identity providers allowed users to create and manage digital identities for multiple services. Platforms like Microsoft's Passport, later rebranded as Microsoft Account, and OpenID attempted to streamline authentication across various websites. However, these early identity federation attempts faced challenges related to user adoption, interoperability, and security vulnerabilities.

The rise of social media platforms brought a significant shift in digital identity management. Companies such as Facebook, Google, and Twitter introduced social login mechanisms, enabling users to authenticate with third-party services using their social media credentials. This approach simplified the user experience by reducing the need to remember multiple passwords while providing service providers with additional user data for personalization and security purposes. However, it also raised privacy concerns, as social login mechanisms often required users to share personal information with multiple organizations, increasing the risk of data misuse and breaches.

With the expansion of cloud computing and mobile technology, digital identity management continued to evolve. Identity and access management (IAM) solutions became essential for enterprises, allowing organizations to control and secure access to applications and systems. Multi-factor authentication (MFA) emerged as a critical security measure, requiring users to provide additional verification factors beyond passwords, such as one-time codes, biometrics, or security keys. These measures significantly enhanced security but also introduced usability challenges, as users had to navigate complex authentication processes.

The introduction of biometrics marked a transformative moment in digital identity evolution. Fingerprint scanning, facial recognition, and voice authentication became increasingly popular, offering more secure and convenient methods for identity verification. Apple's Touch ID and Face ID, as well as Android's biometric authentication features, demonstrated the effectiveness of biometrics in mainstream consumer technology. While biometric authentication enhanced security by reducing reliance on passwords, it also raised ethical concerns about privacy, data storage, and the potential for biometric data misuse.

Decentralized identity solutions began to emerge as a response to growing concerns over centralized identity management. Blockchain technology provided a foundation for self-sovereign identity (SSI), allowing individuals to control their digital identities without relying on centralized authorities. SSI enables users to store and manage their credentials securely, granting access to services without exposing unnecessary personal information. Projects such as the Sovrin Network and the World Wide Web Consortium's Decentralized Identifiers (DIDs) standard aimed to shift control of identity data from corporations to individuals, promoting greater privacy and security.

As digital interactions increased, so did the risks associated with identity fraud, data breaches, and identity theft. Organizations and governments worldwide implemented stricter regulations to protect user data and privacy. The General Data Protection Regulation (GDPR) in Europe and the California Consumer Privacy Act (CCPA) set new standards for data protection, requiring businesses to implement strong security measures and provide users with greater control over their personal information. These regulations pushed identity providers and service providers to adopt more secure authentication mechanisms, such as passwordless authentication, behavioral biometrics, and continuous authentication.

The evolution of digital identity also extended into emerging technologies such as artificial intelligence (AI) and machine learning. AI-powered identity verification systems analyze behavioral patterns, device usage, and contextual factors to assess the legitimacy of authentication requests. Machine learning algorithms enhance fraud detection by identifying anomalies in login attempts, transaction behavior, and biometric scans. These advancements contribute to a more adaptive and resilient digital identity ecosystem, reducing the risks associated with traditional authentication methods.

With the rise of the Internet of Things (IoT), digital identity expanded beyond human users to include devices, applications, and automated systems. IoT devices, ranging from smart home assistants to industrial sensors, require secure identity management to prevent unauthorized access and cyber threats. Identity frameworks such as OAuth and OpenID Connect enable secure authentication and authorization for IoT ecosystems, ensuring that devices interact securely within connected environments.

The future of digital identity will continue to be shaped by technological advancements, regulatory requirements, and user expectations. Concepts such as verifiable credentials, privacy-preserving authentication methods, and identity portability are gaining traction, paving the way for a more secure and user-centric identity landscape. As digital interactions become more integrated into daily life, ensuring the security, privacy, and usability of digital identities will remain a critical challenge for individuals, organizations, and policymakers.

Core Concepts in Identity Management

Identity management is a foundational aspect of modern digital security, enabling organizations and individuals to verify, authenticate, and control access to sensitive resources. As digital interactions grow more complex, identity management has evolved to encompass various frameworks, technologies, and best practices that ensure secure and seamless access control. At its core, identity management revolves around the principles of identification, authentication, authorization, and accountability, all of which play a crucial role in protecting digital assets and personal information.

Identification is the first step in identity management, where an individual or entity presents unique attributes that distinguish them from others. These attributes can include a username, email address, government-issued identification number, or even a biometric identifier such as a fingerprint. Identification alone does not establish trust; it merely provides a label for an entity seeking access to a system or service. To ensure that the presented identity is legitimate, authentication mechanisms are implemented to verify that the user is who they claim to be.

Authentication is the process of proving an identity's validity by verifying credentials against a known set of records. Traditional authentication methods rely on something the user knows, such as a password or PIN. However, as cyber threats have increased, reliance on passwords alone has proven to be insufficient. Modern authentication mechanisms incorporate additional factors, including something the user has, such as a mobile device or security token, and something the user is, such as biometric data. Multi-factor authentication (MFA) enhances security by requiring a combination of these factors, making it significantly harder for unauthorized users to gain access.

Once authentication is successfully completed, the next step is authorization. Authorization determines what level of access an authenticated user has within a system. Access control models define these permissions, ensuring that users only have the rights necessary to perform their tasks. The most common models include role-based access control (RBAC), where permissions are assigned based on predefined roles within an organization, and attribute-based access control (ABAC), which considers user attributes and contextual conditions to determine access rights. Effective authorization mechanisms help prevent unauthorized data access and reduce the risk of privilege escalation attacks.

Accountability is another critical component of identity management, ensuring that all user activities can be traced and monitored. Logging and auditing mechanisms record authentication attempts, access requests, and security events, allowing organizations to detect suspicious activities and respond to potential threats. Accountability is especially important in regulatory compliance, where organizations must demonstrate proper identity governance and adherence to security policies. Strong auditing capabilities enable organizations to maintain transparency and protect against insider threats or external breaches.

Identity lifecycle management is an essential aspect of identity management, overseeing the entire journey of an identity from creation to deactivation. This process includes onboarding new users, modifying access rights as roles change, and deprovisioning accounts when users leave an organization. Automating identity lifecycle management reduces administrative overhead, minimizes human errors, and ensures that access rights are consistently updated based on an individual's responsibilities. Effective lifecycle management prevents issues such as orphaned accounts, which can be exploited by attackers if left unattended.

Federated identity management allows users to access multiple systems and services using a single identity. Instead of creating separate credentials for each platform, users authenticate once and gain access across interconnected applications. Federated identity is commonly implemented through protocols such as Security Assertion Markup Language (SAML) and OpenID Connect, which enable secure identity exchange between different organizations and service providers. Single sign-on (SSO) solutions further streamline this process by reducing the need for repeated logins, enhancing both security and user experience.

Self-sovereign identity (SSI) is an emerging concept in identity management that gives individuals full control over their digital identities. Unlike traditional identity systems that rely on centralized authorities, SSI leverages decentralized technologies such as blockchain to enable users to manage their identity credentials independently. With SSI, users can selectively disclose information to service providers without exposing unnecessary personal details, enhancing privacy and reducing the risk of data breaches. This approach aligns with growing concerns over data sovereignty and user empowerment in digital identity management.

Risk-based authentication (RBA) is a dynamic approach to identity verification that adapts authentication requirements based on contextual risk factors. Instead of enforcing static authentication policies, RBA analyzes factors such as login location, device reputation, and behavioral patterns to determine the likelihood of an identity being compromised. If an authentication attempt is deemed high-risk, additional verification steps may be required. By implementing adaptive security measures, organizations can balance security and usability while mitigating potential threats.

Identity management also extends to non-human entities, including devices, applications, and automated systems. In the Internet of Things (IoT) ecosystem, identity management ensures that connected devices authenticate securely and communicate without unauthorized interference. Machine identities, such as API keys and digital certificates, play a crucial role in securing interactions between applications and cloud services. Effective identity governance for machines is essential in preventing unauthorized access, data leaks, and cyber attacks in distributed computing environments.

The future of identity management continues to be shaped by evolving cybersecurity threats, regulatory requirements, and technological advancements. Organizations must continuously adapt their identity management strategies to address emerging challenges, such as deepfake-based identity fraud, AI-driven attacks, and quantum computing threats. By leveraging modern identity solutions, including passwordless authentication, decentralized identity models, and AI-powered threat detection, organizations can create more secure, user-friendly, and resilient identity management frameworks. The ability to maintain strong identity security while ensuring seamless access will remain a critical priority for businesses, governments, and individuals alike.

Mobile Identity vs. Traditional Identity

The way individuals manage and verify their identity has undergone a significant transformation with the rise of mobile technology. Traditional identity systems have long relied on physical credentials, static authentication methods, and centralized management structures. However, mobile identity has introduced a more dynamic, flexible, and user-centric approach to authentication and access control. As mobile devices become an integral part of daily life, they offer new possibilities for identity management while also presenting unique challenges. Understanding the key differences between mobile identity and traditional identity is essential for evaluating the future of secure digital interactions.

Traditional identity systems are based on the use of physical documents and static authentication methods. Government-issued IDs, passports, social security numbers, and birth certificates have historically been the primary means of identity verification. In the digital realm, traditional identity relies on usernames and passwords, often stored in centralized databases and managed by organizations.

These identity models have been effective for decades, but they suffer from several limitations, including security vulnerabilities, usability challenges, and a lack of flexibility in modern digital ecosystems.

One of the primary weaknesses of traditional identity systems is their reliance on passwords. Password-based authentication has long been the standard for online identity verification, but it has proven to be a major security risk. Users frequently reuse passwords across multiple services, create weak passwords, or fall victim to phishing attacks, making password breaches a common occurrence. Moreover, managing multiple credentials for different platforms can be cumbersome, leading to poor user experience and security trade-offs. While traditional identity systems have incorporated additional security measures such as security questions and one-time passcodes, these methods often introduce friction and are still vulnerable to social engineering attacks.

In contrast, mobile identity leverages the capabilities of modern mobile devices to provide a more seamless and secure authentication experience. Mobile identity refers to the use of smartphones, tablets, and wearable devices as identity verification tools, enabling users to authenticate themselves through various digital methods. Instead of relying solely on passwords, mobile identity incorporates biometric authentication, cryptographic keys, and device-based verification to enhance security. Features such as fingerprint scanning, facial recognition, and behavioral biometrics have made mobile identity not only more secure but also more convenient for users.

One of the defining characteristics of mobile identity is its dynamic nature. Unlike traditional identity, which is often tied to static credentials, mobile identity adapts to user behavior, device context, and environmental factors. Risk-based authentication is commonly used in mobile identity management, analyzing factors such as geolocation, device reputation, and user activity patterns to determine authentication requirements. If an authentication attempt appears suspicious, additional verification steps can be triggered, providing a more adaptive and intelligent security approach.

Another key distinction between mobile identity and traditional identity is the shift from centralized to decentralized identity models.

Traditional identity systems are often managed by a single entity, such as a government agency, financial institution, or corporate IT department. Users must rely on these centralized authorities to verify their identity, often submitting personal information that is stored in large databases. This centralized approach creates significant security risks, as data breaches targeting these databases can expose millions of user identities. Mobile identity, on the other hand, supports decentralized and self-sovereign identity (SSI) models, where users maintain greater control over their credentials. Technologies such as blockchain and decentralized identity protocols enable users to store and manage their digital identities securely on their mobile devices, reducing the need for centralized intermediaries.

The convenience factor of mobile identity is another major advantage over traditional identity systems. Mobile devices are always connected, portable, and equipped with multiple authentication factors, making them ideal for seamless identity verification. Users can authenticate with a simple fingerprint scan or facial recognition check without needing to remember complex passwords or carry physical documents. Mobile identity also enables the use of digital wallets, which can store identity credentials such as driver's licenses, payment cards, and health records in a secure and accessible format. These digital credentials can be verified instantly, reducing the need for manual identity checks in various scenarios, such as airport security, financial transactions, and online account logins.

Despite its advantages, mobile identity also introduces new challenges and security concerns. One of the primary concerns is device security. Unlike traditional identity documents, which are often stored in secure physical locations, mobile identity credentials are vulnerable to theft, malware, and unauthorized access. If a mobile device is lost or compromised, an attacker could potentially gain access to sensitive identity information. To mitigate this risk, mobile identity solutions incorporate features such as remote wipe capabilities, device attestation, and encrypted storage to protect user data.

Privacy is another critical consideration in mobile identity management. While mobile identity solutions offer greater convenience, they also collect and process vast amounts of user data, including location history, biometric information, and behavioral patterns. Ensuring that this data is handled securely and in compliance with privacy regulations is a key challenge for service providers and regulatory bodies. Users must have transparency and control over how their identity data is used, with mechanisms such as consent-based authentication and privacy-preserving technologies playing an important role in addressing these concerns.

The future of identity management will likely involve a hybrid approach that combines elements of both mobile and traditional identity systems. As governments and organizations transition to digital identity solutions, the integration of mobile identity with existing infrastructure will be essential. Many countries are already developing mobile-based national identity programs, allowing citizens to access government services and verify their identity through mobile apps. Similarly, enterprises are adopting mobile identity solutions for workforce authentication, enabling employees to securely access corporate resources from any location.

While traditional identity systems have provided a foundation for authentication and verification, mobile identity represents the next stage of evolution in digital identity management. By leveraging mobile technology, biometrics, and decentralized identity models, mobile identity offers a more secure, user-friendly, and flexible approach to managing identities in the digital age. The transition from traditional to mobile identity will continue to reshape the way individuals interact with online services, financial institutions, and government agencies, ultimately creating a more efficient and secure identity ecosystem.

Authentication Mechanisms

Authentication is the foundation of digital security, ensuring that only authorized users can access systems, applications, and data. As cyber threats become more sophisticated, authentication mechanisms have evolved to balance security and usability. The process of authentication verifies the identity of a user, device, or system before granting access. Various authentication mechanisms exist, each with different levels of security, convenience, and implementation challenges. Understanding these mechanisms is crucial for organizations and individuals aiming to protect sensitive information while maintaining a seamless user experience.

The most common and traditional form of authentication is password-based authentication. Users create a unique combination of characters, numbers, and symbols to prove their identity when logging into a system. While passwords have been widely used for decades, they present significant security vulnerabilities. Many users choose weak passwords, reuse them across multiple accounts, or fall victim to phishing attacks that trick them into revealing their credentials. Additionally, brute force and credential-stuffing attacks make password-only authentication an increasingly ineffective security measure. Organizations have attempted to mitigate these risks by enforcing password complexity rules, requiring periodic password changes, and implementing password managers to help users generate and store secure credentials.

To enhance security, many systems implement multi-factor authentication (MFA), which requires users to provide multiple forms of verification. MFA typically involves a combination of three authentication factors: something the user knows (such as a password or PIN), something the user has (such as a smartphone or security token), and something the user is (such as biometric data). By requiring multiple factors, MFA significantly reduces the likelihood of unauthorized access, as an attacker would need to compromise more than just a password to breach an account.

One of the most widely adopted forms of MFA is two-factor authentication (2FA), which requires a second layer of verification beyond a password. The second factor is often a one-time password (OTP) generated by an authenticator app or sent via SMS. While 2FA provides an additional security layer, SMS-based authentication has vulnerabilities, such as SIM swapping attacks and interception of text messages. Authenticator apps, such as Google Authenticator or Microsoft Authenticator, provide a more secure alternative by generating OTPs locally on the user's device, reducing reliance on external networks.

Biometric authentication is another powerful authentication mechanism that leverages unique physical or behavioral traits to verify identity. Fingerprint scanning, facial recognition, iris scanning, and voice recognition have become popular authentication methods, particularly in mobile devices. Apple's Face ID and Touch ID, as well as Android's biometric authentication features, have demonstrated the efficiency and convenience of biometrics in everyday use. Unlike passwords, biometric credentials cannot be easily forgotten or shared, making them a more secure alternative. However, biometric authentication raises privacy concerns, as biometric data, once compromised, cannot be changed like a password. Secure storage and encryption of biometric data are essential to ensure privacy and security.

Behavioral authentication takes biometric security a step further by analyzing patterns in user behavior to verify identity continuously. This method monitors factors such as typing speed, mouse movements, touchscreen interactions, and even gait patterns to establish a behavioral profile. If a deviation from the established pattern is detected, additional authentication measures may be required. Behavioral authentication offers a seamless user experience, as it does not require explicit user action, but its effectiveness depends on the accuracy of machine learning algorithms and the quality of collected data.

Passwordless authentication is gaining traction as a way to eliminate the risks associated with traditional password-based systems. Instead of requiring a password, users authenticate using biometric data, cryptographic keys, or push notifications. Public key infrastructure (PKI)-based authentication, such as FIDO2 and WebAuthn standards, allows users to log in using a private key stored on their device, eliminating the need for passwords altogether. This approach not only enhances security by reducing the risk of password breaches but also improves user convenience by eliminating the need to remember and manage multiple credentials.

Smart cards and hardware security tokens are another form of authentication that provides strong security for high-risk environments. These physical devices store cryptographic credentials and must be inserted into a computer or tapped against a reader for authentication. Hardware security keys, such as YubiKeys, leverage the FIDO2 standard to provide strong authentication without requiring passwords. Since these devices are resistant to phishing and malware attacks, they are widely used in corporate environments and government institutions where security is a top priority.

Risk-based authentication (RBA) is a dynamic approach that adjusts authentication requirements based on contextual factors. Instead of applying a one-size-fits-all authentication policy, RBA analyzes elements such as login location, device reputation, network conditions, and user behavior to assess the risk level of an authentication attempt. If an attempt appears high-risk, additional authentication steps may be required, such as answering security questions or providing a biometric scan. RBA enhances security while maintaining a frictionless experience for users accessing systems from trusted locations and devices.

Single sign-on (SSO) is a mechanism that allows users to authenticate once and gain access to multiple applications and services without needing to re-enter credentials. SSO is widely used in enterprise environments to simplify authentication across cloud applications, reducing password fatigue and improving productivity. Identity federation protocols such as SAML and OpenID Connect enable secure identity verification between different service providers, allowing users to access third-party platforms with a single authentication session. However, while SSO improves usability, it also creates a single point of failure, meaning that if an attacker compromises an SSO session, they could gain access to multiple accounts.

Continuous authentication is an emerging authentication mechanism that verifies user identity throughout an entire session rather than only at login. Traditional authentication methods only check identity at the beginning of a session, leaving the system vulnerable to session hijacking or unauthorized access after login. Continuous authentication monitors real-time behavioral patterns, device telemetry, and contextual factors to ensure that the authenticated user remains the same throughout the session. If anomalies are detected, the system may request additional verification or automatically terminate the session.

As authentication mechanisms continue to evolve, organizations must adopt a multi-layered approach to security that balances usability, privacy, and risk management. While no single authentication method is foolproof, combining multiple mechanisms such as biometrics, hardware tokens, and behavioral analysis can create a more robust authentication framework. By leveraging modern authentication technologies, organizations and individuals can enhance security while minimizing friction, enabling safer and more convenient access to digital services.

Multi-Factor Authentication (MFA)

In an era where cyber threats are becoming increasingly sophisticated, traditional password-based authentication methods are no longer sufficient to protect sensitive data and user accounts. Multi-Factor Authentication (MFA) has emerged as a crucial security measure that strengthens authentication by requiring users to provide multiple forms of verification before gaining access to a system or service. By combining different authentication factors, MFA significantly reduces the likelihood of unauthorized access, making it one of the most effective defenses against cyberattacks.

MFA is based on the principle of using multiple authentication factors, which generally fall into three categories. The first category is something the user knows, such as a password, PIN, or security question. This factor has been the traditional method of authentication but is often the weakest due to its susceptibility to attacks such as phishing, credential stuffing, and brute force attacks. The second category is something the user has, which can include physical devices like a smartphone, security token, or smart card. This factor ensures that even if an attacker obtains the user's password, they still need access to the physical device to complete authentication. The third category is something the user is, which involves biometric authentication such as fingerprint scanning, facial recognition, voice recognition, or iris scanning. Biometric factors add an extra layer of security because they are unique to each individual and difficult to replicate.

The implementation of MFA varies across different organizations and services, but one of the most common methods is two-factor authentication (2FA). 2FA requires users to provide two distinct authentication factors before accessing an account. A popular form of 2FA is the combination of a password and a one-time password (OTP) sent via SMS or email. While SMS-based 2FA is an improvement over password-only authentication, it has vulnerabilities, including SIM swapping attacks, where cybercriminals take control of a victim's phone number to intercept OTPs. To address these concerns, many organizations encourage the use of authentication apps, such as Google Authenticator, Microsoft Authenticator, or Authy, which generate OTPs on a user's device and are not susceptible to interception.

Security tokens are another widely used MFA method. These can be hardware-based, such as USB security keys, or software-based, like virtual tokens stored on a smartphone. Hardware security keys, such as YubiKeys and FIDO2-compliant devices, offer strong authentication by requiring the user to physically insert the device or tap it against a reader. Since these tokens are not connected to the internet, they are immune to remote attacks such as phishing and keylogging. Many organizations use hardware tokens for high-security environments, including government agencies and financial institutions.

Biometric authentication has gained popularity as a reliable factor in MFA, particularly in mobile devices. Fingerprint sensors, facial recognition, and iris scanners provide seamless and secure authentication without requiring users to remember passwords or carry additional devices. Apple's Face ID and Touch ID, as well as Android's biometric authentication features, have set the standard for secure and convenient authentication. However, biometric authentication comes with its own set of challenges, including concerns about privacy, data storage, and the potential for spoofing attacks using deepfake technology or artificial fingerprints. Secure biometric storage and liveness detection mechanisms are essential to prevent unauthorized access.

Adaptive authentication, also known as risk-based authentication, is an advanced form of MFA that evaluates contextual factors before determining the authentication requirements for a given session. Instead of enforcing the same authentication process for all users, adaptive authentication assesses risk signals such as the user's location, device reputation, login behavior, and IP address. If a login attempt appears suspicious, additional authentication steps are required. For example, if a user logs in from a trusted device in their usual location, the system may allow access with minimal friction. However, if the same user attempts to log in from an unfamiliar device in a different country, they may be prompted to provide biometric authentication or verify their identity through an additional security token.

One of the key benefits of MFA is its ability to mitigate the impact of credential breaches. Even if an attacker successfully obtains a user's password, they would still need the second or third authentication factor to gain access. This makes MFA a powerful defense against phishing attacks, credential stuffing, and brute force attacks. Many data protection regulations, including the General Data Protection Regulation (GDPR) and the Payment Services Directive 2 (PSD2), mandate the use of MFA for certain transactions, especially in banking and financial services, to protect customer accounts from unauthorized access.

Despite its advantages, MFA implementation must balance security and user experience. While adding multiple authentication layers enhances security, it can also introduce friction and inconvenience for users. Some users may find MFA cumbersome, leading to resistance in adoption. Organizations must choose MFA solutions that provide security without negatively impacting usability. The growing adoption of passwordless authentication, which leverages biometric verification, push notifications, and cryptographic keys, aims to reduce user friction while maintaining high security standards.

As cyber threats continue to evolve, MFA remains one of the most effective security measures in identity and access management. Organizations and individuals must prioritize its implementation to safeguard sensitive data, prevent unauthorized access, and reduce the risk of identity theft. With continuous advancements in authentication technology, the future of MFA will likely see the increased adoption of biometric-based authentication, hardware security keys, and AI-driven adaptive security measures. By integrating strong authentication mechanisms into digital security frameworks, businesses and individuals can significantly enhance their protection against modern cyber threats.

Passwordless Authentication

The reliance on passwords as the primary method of authentication has long been a fundamental weakness in digital security. Passwords are prone to theft, reuse, and attacks such as phishing, credential stuffing, and brute force attempts. As cyber threats continue to evolve, organizations and technology providers are shifting towards passwordless authentication, a security model that eliminates passwords entirely in favor of more secure and user-friendly authentication methods. Passwordless authentication enhances security while improving the user experience by removing the burden of remembering and managing complex credentials.

Passwordless authentication is based on the use of alternative factors such as biometrics, cryptographic keys, and device-based authentication methods. Instead of requiring users to input a password, passwordless authentication verifies identity through something they have, such as a registered device or security token, or something they are, such as a fingerprint or facial recognition. This shift reduces the risk of credential-based attacks and strengthens overall security. The primary goal of passwordless authentication is to enhance security without compromising usability, providing a seamless yet highly secure login experience.

One of the most widely adopted forms of passwordless authentication is biometric verification. Modern smartphones, laptops, and other devices now come equipped with fingerprint sensors and facial recognition systems that allow users to authenticate without typing a password. Apple's Face ID and Touch ID, as well as Android's biometric authentication features, have demonstrated how biometrics can provide a frictionless yet highly secure authentication method. Biometrics work by capturing and comparing unique physical characteristics, making it difficult for attackers to impersonate legitimate users. However, biometric authentication also raises concerns about data privacy and the potential misuse of biometric information, making secure storage and encryption of biometric data critical.

Another popular passwordless authentication method is the use of security keys based on public key cryptography. Standards such as FIDO2 and WebAuthn enable users to authenticate using hardware security keys, such as YubiKeys, or built-in device authentication methods like Windows Hello and Apple Passkeys. These methods rely on asymmetric cryptography, where a private key is securely stored on the user's device and never leaves it. When authentication is required, the device signs a challenge using the private key, and the server verifies it using the corresponding public key. Since there are no passwords to steal, passwordless authentication using cryptographic keys eliminates the risks associated with phishing and credential theft.

Push notification-based authentication is another widely used passwordless approach. When a user attempts to log in, a push notification is sent to their registered mobile device, prompting them to approve or deny the authentication request. This method ensures that only the rightful owner of the device can authenticate, making it a secure and convenient alternative to passwords. Services such as Microsoft Authenticator and Duo Security leverage push notifications to enable passwordless logins while maintaining strong security measures. This approach also benefits from real-time authentication, allowing users to deny unauthorized login attempts instantly.

Passkeys, an emerging passwordless authentication technology, are gaining traction as a replacement for traditional passwords. Passkeys, developed based on FIDO standards, allow users to authenticate across devices and platforms without needing a password. When a user sets up a passkey, the system generates a cryptographic key pair, securely storing the private key on the user's device. When logging in, authentication is completed using biometrics or a PIN, with the device handling the cryptographic exchange. Unlike passwords, passkeys cannot be phished, stolen, or reused, making them one of the most secure authentication methods available.

Passwordless authentication also plays a significant role in enterprise security and workforce identity management. Organizations are increasingly adopting passwordless solutions to secure employee access to corporate resources while reducing IT overhead associated with password resets and credential management. By implementing single sign-on (SSO) solutions with passwordless authentication, businesses can improve security while streamlining access to applications and services. Passwordless authentication also enhances compliance with data protection regulations by reducing the risks of password-related breaches and unauthorized access.

Despite its advantages, passwordless authentication faces challenges related to adoption, compatibility, and user acceptance. One of the main hurdles is the need for widespread support across different platforms, applications, and devices. While modern operating systems and browsers have integrated passwordless authentication standards, many legacy systems and applications still rely on passwords, making a full transition difficult. Additionally, users who are accustomed to password-based logins may be hesitant to adopt new authentication methods, requiring organizations to invest in education and training to facilitate adoption.

Security considerations also play a crucial role in the implementation of passwordless authentication. While eliminating passwords significantly reduces phishing and credential theft, passwordless authentication is not immune to attacks. For example, biometric authentication systems can be targeted by spoofing techniques such as deepfakes or synthetic fingerprints. Similarly, device-based authentication methods may be compromised if an attacker gains access to a user's registered device. To address these risks, organizations must implement multi-layered security measures, including biometric liveness detection, device attestation, and contextual authentication analysis.

The shift towards passwordless authentication represents a major advancement in digital security, offering a more secure, user-friendly alternative to traditional password-based systems. As adoption continues to grow, passwordless authentication will become the standard for securing online accounts, enterprise systems, and digital transactions. By leveraging biometrics, cryptographic keys, and push-based authentication methods, organizations and individuals can significantly enhance security while simplifying the authentication process. The transition to a passwordless future will require collaboration between technology providers, businesses, and users, but its potential to eliminate password-related vulnerabilities makes it one of the most promising innovations in identity management.

Biometrics and Mobile Identity

Biometric authentication has revolutionized the way individuals verify their identity, offering a secure and convenient alternative to traditional password-based authentication methods. With the rise of mobile identity, biometrics have become an essential component of digital security, enabling users to authenticate themselves using unique biological traits. Mobile devices, such as smartphones and tablets, now incorporate sophisticated biometric authentication mechanisms, making identity verification faster, more reliable, and resistant to common cyber threats. As the adoption of mobile biometrics continues to grow, it is transforming how people access services, conduct financial transactions, and protect sensitive data.

Biometrics are based on the concept that each individual possesses distinct physical or behavioral characteristics that can be used for identity verification. Unlike passwords, which can be forgotten, stolen, or compromised, biometric traits are inherently unique to each person, making them a highly secure authentication method. The most commonly used biometric authentication methods in mobile identity include fingerprint recognition, facial recognition, iris scanning, and voice recognition. These technologies leverage advanced sensors and artificial intelligence (AI) algorithms to analyze and compare biometric data, ensuring accurate and secure identity verification.

Fingerprint recognition is one of the earliest and most widely adopted forms of mobile biometric authentication. With the introduction of fingerprint sensors in smartphones, such as Apple's Touch ID and Android's biometric fingerprint authentication, users can unlock their devices, authorize payments, and access secure applications with a simple touch. Fingerprint authentication works by capturing an image of the user's fingerprint and converting it into a digital template. This template is then securely stored and used for future authentication attempts. Because fingerprints are unique and remain relatively stable over a person's lifetime, this method offers a high level of security and reliability. However, fingerprint recognition can be affected by factors such as dirt, moisture, or injuries on the finger, which may interfere with the sensor's accuracy.

Facial recognition has gained significant popularity with the advent of advanced mobile authentication technologies such as Apple's Face ID and Android's facial recognition systems. This technology uses cameras and AI-driven algorithms to analyze facial features, including the shape of the eyes, nose, and jawline, to create a digital facial signature. Unlike fingerprint recognition, which requires physical contact with a sensor, facial recognition enables contactless authentication, enhancing convenience and hygiene. Modern facial recognition systems use depth-sensing cameras and infrared technology to prevent spoofing attempts, such as using a photograph or video to bypass authentication. Despite its advantages, facial recognition raises concerns about privacy, as biometric facial data is often stored on devices or in centralized databases, making it a potential target for cyberattacks.

Iris scanning is another highly secure biometric authentication method, although it is less commonly used in mobile devices compared to fingerprint and facial recognition. This technology captures high-resolution images of the user's iris and analyzes unique patterns within the eye. Iris recognition is extremely accurate, as the iris pattern remains stable throughout a person's life and is difficult to replicate. Some high-end smartphones have incorporated iris scanning for enhanced security, particularly in banking and government applications. However, the adoption of iris scanning in mobile devices has been slower due to the need for specialized sensors and the requirement for users to align their eyes precisely with the scanner.

Voice recognition is a biometric authentication method that analyzes a user's vocal characteristics, including tone, pitch, and speech patterns, to verify identity. Mobile devices with voice recognition capabilities enable hands-free authentication, allowing users to unlock devices, authorize transactions, and access secure applications through voice commands. Voice authentication is particularly useful for accessibility, enabling users with disabilities to interact with mobile systems more efficiently. However, voice recognition is susceptible to background noise, voice changes due to illness, and spoofing attempts using recorded audio, requiring additional security measures such as liveness detection and anti-spoofing technologies.

One of the key advantages of biometric authentication in mobile identity is its seamless integration with mobile security frameworks. Unlike traditional authentication methods that rely on passwords or PINs, which can be easily compromised, biometrics provide an additional layer of security that enhances identity protection. Many mobile devices now combine biometric authentication with cryptographic security mechanisms, such as Secure Enclave in Apple devices and Trusted Execution Environment (TEE) in Android devices. These secure storage solutions ensure that biometric data is encrypted and stored locally on the device, reducing the risk of unauthorized access or data breaches.

Despite its advantages, biometric authentication also presents challenges related to security, privacy, and ethical concerns. One of the main concerns is the risk of biometric data breaches. Unlike passwords, which can be changed if compromised, biometric traits are permanent and cannot be altered. If a hacker gains access to biometric data, it can be used for identity fraud or unauthorized access to sensitive accounts. To mitigate this risk, biometric authentication systems must implement strong encryption, secure storage methods, and anti-spoofing techniques to prevent fraudulent activities.

Privacy concerns also arise with the widespread use of biometric authentication in mobile identity. As governments, financial institutions, and technology companies increasingly rely on biometric data for identity verification, questions about data ownership, consent, and surveillance become more critical. Regulations such as the General Data Protection Regulation (GDPR) and the California Consumer Privacy Act (CCPA) require organizations to obtain user consent before collecting and storing biometric data. Ensuring compliance with these regulations is essential for protecting user privacy and maintaining trust in biometric authentication systems.

The future of biometrics in mobile identity is expected to see further advancements in AI-driven authentication, multimodal biometrics, and decentralized identity solutions. AI-powered authentication systems can enhance biometric security by continuously analyzing user behavior and detecting anomalies that may indicate fraudulent activities. Multimodal biometrics, which combine multiple authentication methods such as fingerprint and facial recognition, can improve accuracy and security by requiring multiple verification factors. Additionally, decentralized identity models, which allow users to store and control their biometric data on their devices rather than in centralized databases, offer greater privacy and security.

As biometric authentication continues to evolve, it will play an increasingly vital role in securing mobile identities and enhancing digital interactions. The combination of biometric authentication, AI-driven security mechanisms, and privacy-preserving technologies will shape the future of mobile identity management, providing users with a secure, seamless, and user-friendly authentication experience.

Identity Verification Techniques

Identity verification is a crucial process in digital security, ensuring that individuals, organizations, and systems are accurately identified before being granted access to sensitive information or services. As online transactions, mobile services, and digital interactions continue to increase, identity verification techniques have evolved to provide higher levels of security while maintaining user convenience. These techniques range from traditional document-based verification methods to advanced biometric and AI-driven solutions, helping organizations mitigate fraud, prevent identity theft, and comply with regulatory requirements.

One of the oldest and most widely used identity verification methods is document-based verification. This technique requires individuals to present official identification documents such as passports, driver's licenses, or national ID cards. In many cases, these documents are scanned or photographed using a mobile device or webcam, and their authenticity is verified by comparing them to government-issued templates or security features such as holograms and watermarks. While document-based verification is effective for initial identity registration, it has limitations, including the risk of forged documents and the need for manual review, which can slow down the verification process.

To enhance document verification, optical character recognition (OCR) technology and artificial intelligence (AI) are now widely used to automate the extraction of identity information from documents. OCR scans the text from a document and converts it into digital data, while AI algorithms analyze features such as fonts, colors, and embedded security markers to detect forgery attempts. Some systems also use liveness detection techniques to verify that the document is being presented by a real person rather than a static image or a manipulated document. These automated approaches reduce human intervention, increase verification speed, and improve accuracy.

Biometric verification has become one of the most reliable identity verification techniques in modern digital systems. Biometrics use unique physical or behavioral characteristics, such as fingerprints, facial recognition, iris scanning, or voice recognition, to confirm a person's identity. Many organizations, particularly in banking and healthcare, use biometric verification to enhance security while improving the user experience. Mobile devices now include built-in biometric sensors, allowing users to authenticate themselves easily through fingerprint scanning or facial recognition. Unlike passwords or documents, biometric data is difficult to forge or steal, making it a more secure verification method.

Facial recognition technology is a widely adopted biometric verification method, often used in mobile identity verification. This technique captures and analyzes unique facial features to create a biometric template that can be matched against stored data. AI-powered facial recognition systems incorporate liveness detection to prevent spoofing attempts, such as using a photograph or video to bypass authentication. Many financial institutions and digital service providers require users to take a selfie while following instructions, such as blinking or turning their head, to ensure that the verification process is not being manipulated. However, concerns about privacy and biometric data security remain, as facial recognition systems must handle sensitive user data responsibly.

Fingerprint verification is another biometric technique commonly used for identity verification. This method requires users to scan their fingerprints using a biometric sensor, which then compares the captured data to a pre-registered template. Fingerprint verification is widely used in mobile authentication, secure transactions, and access control systems. The advantage of this method is its high accuracy and ease of use. However, fingerprint recognition can sometimes be affected by environmental factors such as moisture, dirt, or injuries, which may interfere with the sensor's ability to capture a clear fingerprint.

Another emerging identity verification technique is voice recognition, which analyzes an individual's vocal characteristics, such as pitch, tone, and pronunciation patterns. Voice-based verification is particularly useful for hands-free authentication in mobile applications, call centers, and smart assistants. The technology creates a unique voiceprint for each user, allowing them to authenticate themselves simply by speaking a specific phrase. While voice recognition provides a convenient and non-intrusive verification method, it can be vulnerable to environmental noise, voice alterations due to illness, and spoofing attacks using recorded audio. To mitigate these risks, advanced voice recognition systems incorporate AI-based fraud detection and liveness analysis.

Behavioral biometrics is an innovative identity verification technique that continuously analyzes user behavior to verify identity. Unlike traditional authentication methods that require active user participation, behavioral biometrics operate in the background, analyzing patterns such as typing speed, mouse movements, touchscreen interactions, and gait. These behavioral traits are unique to each individual and difficult to replicate, making them an effective form of identity verification. Behavioral biometrics are often used in fraud detection systems, where they help identify suspicious activity by comparing a user's real-time behavior to their historical patterns.

Knowledge-based verification (KBV) is another common method used for identity verification, particularly in financial transactions and online account recovery. KBV requires users to answer personal questions based on their history, such as their mother's maiden name, previous addresses, or details about past transactions. While KBV adds an extra layer of security, it has become increasingly unreliable due to the widespread availability of personal data on the internet and social media. Cybercriminals can often find answers to security questions through data breaches or social engineering, reducing the effectiveness of this verification method.

Multi-factor verification (MFV) combines multiple identity verification techniques to enhance security. Rather than relying on a single factor, such as a password or fingerprint, MFV requires users to provide at least two different forms of verification. For example, a banking app may require users to scan their ID document, verify their face using facial recognition, and confirm their phone number through an SMS code. This layered approach significantly reduces the likelihood of fraud and identity theft, as attackers must bypass multiple verification steps to gain unauthorized access.

As regulatory requirements and cybersecurity threats continue to evolve, identity verification techniques must also adapt to provide stronger security while maintaining a seamless user experience. Governments and businesses are investing in AI-driven identity verification solutions that can analyze vast amounts of data in real-time, detect anomalies, and prevent fraud. The use of blockchain technology is also being explored to create decentralized identity verification systems, where users have greater control over their personal information and can verify their identity without relying on centralized databases.

The future of identity verification will likely involve a combination of AI-powered fraud detection, biometric authentication, and privacy-preserving technologies. As digital interactions become more integrated into daily life, ensuring the accuracy, security, and efficiency of identity verification techniques will be essential for protecting individuals and organizations from identity fraud, cyber threats, and unauthorized access.

Zero Trust and Mobile Security

The traditional security model relied on the assumption that once a user or device was inside a corporate network, it could be trusted. However, with the rise of mobile devices, remote work, and cloud computing, this perimeter-based security approach has become obsolete. Cyber threats are more sophisticated than ever, and attackers are constantly finding ways to exploit vulnerabilities, making it crucial to adopt a more resilient security framework. The Zero Trust security model has emerged as a modern approach that eliminates the concept of inherent trust and instead verifies every access request, whether inside or outside an organization's network. When applied to mobile security, Zero Trust provides a robust defense against unauthorized access, malware, and data breaches, ensuring that mobile users and their devices are continuously authenticated and monitored.

Zero Trust operates on the fundamental principle of "never trust, always verify." Unlike traditional security models that assume trust within a network, Zero Trust enforces strict identity verification, device security checks, and least-privilege access for all users and devices. This means that every request for access must be authenticated and authorized before being granted, regardless of whether the request originates from inside or outside the organization. Mobile security benefits greatly from this approach, as mobile devices frequently connect to multiple networks, including unsecured public Wi-Fi, which increases the risk of cyber threats.

A key component of Zero Trust in mobile security is strong identity verification. Mobile devices are often used for work-related tasks, accessing corporate data, emails, and cloud services. Ensuring that only authorized users can access these resources requires continuous authentication and adaptive security measures. Multi-factor authentication (MFA) plays a critical role in Zero Trust, requiring users to verify their identity using a combination of factors such as passwords, biometric authentication, and security tokens. However, traditional MFA methods may not be sufficient in dynamic mobile environments. Risk-based authentication, which assesses factors such as login location, device type, and user behavior, enhances security by applying different authentication requirements based on contextual risk.

Device security is another crucial element of Zero Trust in mobile environments. Since mobile devices are highly portable, they are more susceptible to theft, loss, and unauthorized access. Organizations implementing a Zero Trust approach must ensure that only secure, compliant devices can access corporate networks and sensitive data. Mobile device management (MDM) and endpoint detection and response (EDR) solutions help enforce security policies, such as device encryption, remote wipe capabilities, and application restrictions. These measures ensure that even if a mobile device is compromised, sensitive data remains protected.

Network security is also a significant challenge in mobile security, as users frequently switch between different networks, including public Wi-Fi, mobile data, and home networks. Traditional perimeter-based security models fail to provide adequate protection against threats that exploit unsecured networks. In a Zero Trust framework, network security is enhanced by implementing micro-segmentation and least-privilege access. Micro-segmentation ensures that users and devices can only access the specific resources they need, reducing the potential attack surface. Additionally, secure access service edge (SASE) solutions integrate Zero Trust principles with cloud-based network security, ensuring encrypted connections and real-time threat monitoring for mobile users.

Another important aspect of Zero Trust and mobile security is continuous monitoring and anomaly detection. Unlike traditional security models that rely on one-time authentication at login, Zero Trust continuously evaluates user behavior and device activity to detect potential threats. Artificial intelligence (AI) and machine learning (ML) play a vital role in identifying suspicious activities, such as unusual login attempts, changes in device location, or unexpected access requests. By leveraging AI-driven analytics, organizations can detect and respond to security incidents in real time, preventing potential breaches before they occur.

Zero Trust also emphasizes the importance of secure application access. Mobile users frequently access corporate applications, cloud services, and collaboration tools, making it essential to secure these interactions. Zero Trust network access (ZTNA) replaces traditional virtual private networks (VPNs) by providing secure, granular access to applications without exposing the entire network. Unlike VPNs, which grant full network access once a user is authenticated, ZTNA enforces least-privilege access, ensuring that users can only access the applications and data they are authorized for. This reduces the risk of lateral movement within a network if an attacker compromises a user's credentials.

Data protection is another critical component of Zero Trust in mobile security. Mobile devices store and transmit vast amounts of sensitive information, making them prime targets for data breaches. Organizations implementing Zero Trust must enforce data encryption, both at rest and in transit, to protect sensitive information from unauthorized access. Additionally, data loss prevention (DLP) solutions help monitor and control the movement of data, preventing unauthorized sharing or exfiltration of corporate information.

The adoption of Zero Trust in mobile security also aligns with regulatory compliance requirements. Many industries, including finance, healthcare, and government, must adhere to strict data protection regulations such as the General Data Protection Regulation (GDPR), the California Consumer Privacy Act (CCPA), and the Health Insurance Portability and Accountability Act (HIPAA). Implementing Zero Trust helps organizations meet these regulatory requirements by enforcing strong identity verification, data encryption, and access controls, reducing the risk of compliance violations and financial penalties.

Despite its many advantages, the implementation of Zero Trust in mobile security comes with challenges. Organizations must ensure that Zero Trust policies do not introduce excessive friction that disrupts user productivity. Striking the right balance between security and usability requires careful planning, user education, and the adoption of technologies that provide seamless authentication while maintaining strong security measures. Additionally, integrating Zero Trust with existing IT infrastructure and legacy systems may require significant investment in security solutions and policy updates.

The increasing adoption of mobile devices for work and personal use has made Zero Trust a necessary security framework in today's digital landscape. Traditional security models are no longer effective in protecting against modern cyber threats, and organizations must embrace a Zero Trust approach to secure their mobile workforce. By continuously verifying identity, monitoring device security, enforcing least-privilege access, and securing network connections, Zero Trust provides a comprehensive security strategy that ensures mobile users and their data remain protected in an evolving threat environment.

Identity Providers and Federated Identity

As digital services expand across multiple platforms, users often need to authenticate themselves on various applications and systems. Managing multiple credentials for different services is not only inconvenient but also increases security risks. Identity providers (IdPs) and federated identity solutions have emerged as key components of modern identity and access management (IAM), streamlining authentication processes while enhancing security. These solutions enable users to access multiple services with a single set of credentials, reducing password fatigue and mitigating risks associated with credential reuse and phishing attacks.

An identity provider (IdP) is a trusted entity that manages and verifies user identities. Instead of requiring users to create separate accounts for each application, an IdP provides a centralized authentication mechanism that allows users to sign in once and gain access to multiple services. IdPs store and manage identity attributes such as usernames, passwords, email addresses, and multi-factor authentication (MFA) preferences. When a user attempts to access a service that relies on an IdP, the service redirects the authentication request to the IdP, which then verifies the user's credentials and grants or denies access based on predefined policies.

There are different types of identity providers, including enterprise IdPs, social IdPs, and cloud-based IdPs. Enterprise IdPs, such as Microsoft Active Directory (AD) and Okta, are commonly used in corporate environments to manage employee access to internal applications and services. These IdPs integrate with single sign-on (SSO) solutions, allowing employees to authenticate once and access multiple enterprise resources securely. Social IdPs, such as Google, Facebook, and Apple, enable users to authenticate using their social media credentials, simplifying access to consumer applications and reducing the need to create new accounts. Cloud-based IdPs, such as Amazon Cognito and Autho, provide identity management as a service, allowing businesses to integrate authentication and user management into their applications without maintaining on-premises infrastructure.

Federated identity builds upon the concept of identity providers by enabling interoperability between multiple organizations and service providers. In a federated identity system, users can authenticate with one organization and gain access to services provided by other organizations within the federation. This approach eliminates the need for users to create separate accounts for each service while maintaining a high level of security and trust between entities. Federated identity is widely used in industries such as healthcare, education, and government, where multiple organizations need to share access to common resources securely.

One of the most common protocols used in federated identity management is Security Assertion Markup Language (SAML). SAML is an XML-based standard that enables secure exchange of authentication and authorization data between IdPs and service providers. When a user attempts to access a federated service, the service provider redirects the authentication request to the IdP, which then generates a SAML assertion containing the user's identity attributes. This assertion is sent back to the service provider, which verifies its authenticity and grants access based on the included attributes. SAML is widely used in enterprise environments to enable SSO across multiple business applications.

Another important protocol for federated identity is OpenID Connect (OIDC), which is built on top of the OAuth 2.0 authorization framework. Unlike SAML, which relies on XML, OIDC uses JSON Web Tokens (JWTs) to facilitate authentication. OIDC is commonly used in modern web and mobile applications, enabling users to sign in with identity providers such as Google, Microsoft, and Apple. The lightweight nature of OIDC makes it more suitable for cloud-based and mobile applications, where fast and efficient authentication is required.

Federated identity also plays a crucial role in single sign-on (SSO) solutions, which allow users to authenticate once and access multiple applications without needing to re-enter their credentials. SSO reduces the need for users to manage multiple passwords, enhancing both security and user experience. Enterprise SSO solutions integrate with identity providers to provide seamless authentication across corporate applications, reducing IT overhead associated with password resets and account management. However, SSO introduces a potential security risk: if an attacker compromises a user's credentials, they could gain access to multiple services. To mitigate this risk, organizations often implement MFA and conditional access policies to strengthen authentication security.

One of the key challenges in federated identity management is establishing trust between different organizations and service providers. Federations require agreements and policies that define how identity attributes are managed, shared, and verified. Organizations must ensure that identity data is protected against unauthorized access and comply with privacy regulations such as the General Data Protection Regulation (GDPR) and the California Consumer Privacy Act (CCPA). These regulations require identity providers and service providers to implement strong security measures, including encryption, consent management, and data minimization practices.

Decentralized identity is an emerging concept that aims to give users greater control over their digital identities while reducing reliance on centralized identity providers. In a decentralized identity model, users manage their own identity credentials using blockchain-based technologies and self-sovereign identity (SSI) solutions. Instead of relying on a single IdP, users store their identity attributes in a digital wallet and share only the necessary information with service providers. Verifiable credentials, which are cryptographically signed identity attributes, allow users to prove their identity without disclosing excessive personal data. Decentralized identity initiatives, such as the World Wide Web Consortium (W3C) Decentralized Identifiers (DIDs) and the Sovrin Network, are working towards creating a more privacy-focused and user-centric identity ecosystem.

Despite its advantages, federated identity management faces several challenges, including interoperability issues, security risks, and user adoption. Different identity providers and service providers may implement authentication protocols in varying ways, leading to compatibility issues. Organizations must also ensure that their federated identity systems are protected against identity fraud, phishing attacks, and account takeovers. Continuous monitoring, risk-based authentication, and AI-driven fraud detection are essential to maintaining the security of federated identity environments.

As digital interactions continue to grow, identity providers and federated identity solutions will remain fundamental to secure access management. By enabling seamless authentication, reducing password-related risks, and fostering trust between organizations, these technologies play a vital role in modern identity security. Whether through traditional IdPs, federated identity protocols, or decentralized identity models, the evolution of identity management will continue to shape the future of digital security and user authentication.

OAuth and OpenID Connect

In the modern digital landscape, secure and seamless authentication is essential for protecting user data and enabling access to online services. Traditional authentication mechanisms, such as username and password-based logins, present security risks due to password reuse, phishing attacks, and credential theft. To address these issues, modern authentication protocols like OAuth and OpenID Connect (OIDC) have become widely adopted to facilitate secure authorization and authentication. These protocols allow users to access multiple services without exposing their credentials to third-party applications, improving both security and user experience.

OAuth (Open Authorization) is an open standard for delegated authorization that allows applications to access user resources without exposing passwords. Originally developed for API access control, OAuth enables users to grant third-party applications permission to access their data stored on another service. For example, when a user links a social media account to a third-party app, OAuth facilitates secure access without requiring the user to share their login credentials. This approach enhances security by reducing the need for direct credential sharing while giving users control over which applications can access their data.

The OAuth framework consists of several key components: the resource owner, the client, the authorization server, and the resource server. The resource owner is the user who grants permission for data access. The client is the third-party application requesting access to the user's data. The authorization server authenticates the user and issues an access token to the client. Finally, the resource server hosts the protected data and grants access based on the validity of the access token. This separation of roles ensures a secure authorization flow without exposing user credentials to untrusted parties.

OAuth operates through different grant types, which define how an application obtains an access token. The most commonly used grant type is the authorization code flow, which involves redirecting the user to an authorization server, obtaining a temporary authorization code, and exchanging it for an access token. This method is considered the most secure because it minimizes exposure of sensitive data in client-side applications. Another widely used grant type is the client credentials flow, which allows machine-to-machine authentication without user involvement, commonly used for API integrations. Implicit flow and password grant type were previously used in some applications but have been largely deprecated due to security concerns.

While OAuth is a powerful framework for authorization, it does not provide authentication on its own. This limitation led to the development of OpenID Connect (OIDC), which extends OAuth 2.0 to include authentication capabilities. OIDC allows users to authenticate with an identity provider (IdP) and obtain identity information in a standardized format. It enables single sign-on (SSO) functionality, allowing users to log in once and access multiple services without re-entering credentials.

OIDC introduces the concept of an ID token, a JSON Web Token (JWT) that contains claims about the authenticated user. Unlike OAuth's access token, which grants access to protected resources, the ID token provides identity information, such as the user's name, email, and authentication status. The authentication flow in OIDC closely resembles OAuth's authorization code flow, but with the additional step of issuing an ID token alongside the access token. This allows applications to verify user identity without relying on traditional password-based authentication.

The security benefits of OIDC make it an essential protocol for modern authentication. By leveraging public key cryptography, OIDC ensures that ID tokens cannot be tampered with or forged. Additionally, OIDC supports advanced security mechanisms such as Proof Key for Code Exchange (PKCE), which protects against code interception attacks in mobile and single-page applications. These security measures make OIDC a preferred choice for implementing secure authentication in web and mobile applications.

One of the most significant advantages of OAuth and OIDC is their role in enabling federated identity management. With OIDC, users can authenticate with an identity provider like Google, Microsoft, or Facebook and gain access to multiple third-party applications without creating separate credentials for each service. This federated authentication model enhances user convenience while reducing the risks associated with password-based authentication. Organizations implementing OIDC-based SSO solutions benefit from improved security, streamlined user management, and reduced IT support overhead.

Despite their advantages, OAuth and OIDC implementations must be carefully designed to prevent security vulnerabilities. Poorly implemented OAuth flows can lead to token leakage, allowing attackers to gain unauthorized access to user data. Phishing attacks targeting OAuth authorization flows can trick users into granting permissions to malicious applications. To mitigate these risks, organizations must enforce strong security practices, such as using short-lived access tokens, implementing token revocation mechanisms, and validating redirect URIs to prevent open redirect attacks.

OAuth and OIDC are widely used across various industries and applications. Social login systems, enterprise SSO solutions, mobile authentication, and API security all rely on these protocols to manage authentication and authorization securely. As digital services continue to expand, the adoption of OAuth and OIDC will play a critical role in ensuring secure and seamless identity management. By leveraging these protocols, organizations can enhance security, reduce reliance on passwords, and provide users with a more convenient and secure authentication experience.

Single Sign-On (SSO) for Mobile

As mobile devices become the primary means of accessing digital services, users expect seamless and secure authentication across multiple applications. Single Sign-On (SSO) has emerged as a critical solution for enhancing the mobile user experience while maintaining strong security standards. SSO allows users to authenticate once and gain access to multiple applications without needing to re-enter credentials. This approach reduces password fatigue, improves security, and streamlines access management for enterprises and service providers.

Mobile authentication presents unique challenges compared to traditional desktop environments. Users frequently switch between applications, networks, and devices, increasing the need for an authentication system that provides continuous and secure access. Unlike desktop-based authentication, where cookies and session tokens can persist more easily, mobile SSO must account for factors such as app sandboxing, limited session persistence, and network security risks. By leveraging industry-standard authentication protocols such as OAuth 2.0, OpenID Connect (OIDC), and Security Assertion Markup Language (SAML), mobile SSO provides a scalable and secure way to manage authentication across applications.

One of the primary benefits of SSO for mobile is its ability to eliminate the need for multiple passwords. Traditionally, users must remember and enter different credentials for each application, increasing the likelihood of weak passwords, credential reuse, and phishing attacks. With SSO, users authenticate once with a trusted identity provider (IdP), which then issues an authentication token that can be used to access multiple applications. This approach not only enhances security by reducing password exposure but also improves user experience by minimizing authentication friction.

The mobile SSO process typically begins with a user signing in to an identity provider using a secure authentication method, such as biometrics, a password, or multi-factor authentication (MFA). Once authenticated, the IdP generates a session token or an authentication token, which is then passed to authorized applications. These applications validate the token with the IdP and allow access without requiring the user to enter credentials again. The token is stored securely on the mobile device and can be used for future authentication requests until it expires or the session is revoked.

OAuth 2.0 and OpenID Connect are the most commonly used protocols for mobile SSO. OAuth 2.0 provides a framework for secure delegated access, allowing mobile applications to authenticate users through an identity provider without directly handling credentials. OpenID Connect extends OAuth 2.0 by adding an identity layer, enabling applications to retrieve user identity information through ID tokens. This combination allows mobile applications to verify user identities efficiently while maintaining security best practices.

Security Assertion Markup Language (SAML) is another protocol used for SSO, particularly in enterprise environments. SAML enables secure authentication exchanges between identity providers and service providers using XML-based assertions. While SAML is widely used for web-based SSO, it is less commonly implemented in mobile applications due to its reliance on browser-based authentication flows. However, many enterprises integrate SAML with OAuth or OIDC to enable mobile SSO while maintaining compatibility with existing authentication infrastructures.

Device security plays a crucial role in mobile SSO implementations. Unlike traditional workstations, mobile devices are more vulnerable to loss, theft, and malware attacks. Organizations implementing mobile SSO must ensure that authentication tokens and session data are securely stored on the device. Secure storage mechanisms, such as Android Keystore and iOS Secure Enclave, help protect sensitive authentication data from unauthorized access. Additionally, mobile SSO solutions often incorporate device attestation techniques to verify the integrity of the mobile device before granting access to corporate resources.

Federated identity management is often integrated with mobile SSO to enable seamless cross-platform authentication. With federated identity, users can authenticate with one organization and gain access to services provided by other trusted entities. This approach is widely used in enterprise environments, where employees access multiple cloud-based applications using corporate credentials. By leveraging identity federation protocols such as SAML, OAuth, and OIDC, organizations can ensure consistent authentication experiences across both mobile and web platforms.

While mobile SSO offers significant security and usability benefits, it also introduces potential risks if not implemented correctly. One of the primary concerns is token theft or session hijacking. If an attacker gains access to an authentication token stored on a compromised device, they can use it to impersonate the user. To mitigate this risk, organizations must enforce security measures such as short-lived tokens, refresh tokens with secure re-authentication, and continuous monitoring for suspicious login activities.

Another challenge in mobile SSO is balancing security and usability. While strong authentication mechanisms enhance security, excessive authentication prompts can frustrate users and hinder productivity. Adaptive authentication solutions help address this issue by dynamically adjusting authentication requirements based on contextual factors such as device reputation, geolocation, and user behavior. If a login attempt is deemed low-risk, the system may allow seamless authentication with minimal friction, while high-risk attempts trigger additional verification steps.

Mobile SSO also plays a key role in enabling Zero Trust security models, where no device or user is inherently trusted. In a Zero Trust framework, mobile SSO is combined with conditional access policies to enforce strict authentication and authorization rules. These policies evaluate factors such as user identity, device compliance, network security posture, and behavioral analytics before granting access. By integrating mobile SSO with Zero Trust principles, organizations can enhance security while providing a frictionless authentication experience for legitimate users.

As mobile authentication continues to evolve, innovations such as passwordless authentication and decentralized identity are expected to enhance mobile SSO solutions. Passwordless authentication methods, including biometric authentication and FIDO2-based security keys, reduce reliance on traditional passwords, further strengthening mobile security. Decentralized identity models, which allow users to control their authentication credentials without relying on a central authority, offer new possibilities for mobile SSO while improving user privacy.

With the increasing adoption of mobile devices for both personal and enterprise use, SSO has become an essential component of modern identity management. By reducing password-related risks, streamlining authentication processes, and enhancing security, mobile SSO provides a seamless and secure way for users to access multiple applications across different platforms. Organizations must carefully implement SSO solutions using best practices, secure authentication protocols, and adaptive security measures to ensure a balance between usability and strong security.

Mobile Identity in Enterprise Environments

As enterprises increasingly embrace digital transformation, mobile identity has become a cornerstone of secure access management in corporate environments. Employees now rely on mobile devices to access corporate applications, communicate with colleagues, and manage business processes. While this mobility enhances productivity and flexibility, it also introduces new security challenges that require robust identity and access management (IAM) strategies. Mobile identity in enterprise environments involves verifying user identities, enforcing access controls, and ensuring that corporate data remains secure across various devices and locations.

The adoption of mobile identity in enterprises is driven by the shift towards remote work, bring-your-own-device (BYOD) policies, and cloud-based applications. Employees expect seamless and secure access to corporate resources from their smartphones, tablets, and laptops, whether they are in the office, working from home, or traveling. To accommodate this shift, enterprises implement mobile identity solutions that enable secure authentication, device management, and real-time access controls. These solutions not only enhance security but also improve user experience by reducing authentication friction and enabling single sign-on (SSO) across enterprise applications.

One of the key aspects of mobile identity in enterprise environments is multi-factor authentication (MFA). Traditional password-based authentication is no longer sufficient to protect corporate systems, as passwords are vulnerable to phishing attacks, credential theft, and brute force attacks. Enterprises now require employees to use MFA, which combines something they know (password), something they have (smartphone or security token), and something they are (biometric authentication). Mobile devices play a central role in MFA by serving as the second authentication factor through push notifications, one-time passwords (OTPs), and biometric verification.

Identity and access management (IAM) solutions help enterprises manage mobile identity by enforcing security policies, monitoring user access, and integrating authentication methods. These solutions provide centralized control over user identities, ensuring that employees can only access resources they are authorized to use. IAM platforms integrate with enterprise applications, cloud services, and on-premises systems, allowing organizations to implement consistent identity policies across all platforms. Mobile IAM capabilities include user provisioning, role-based access control (RBAC), and real-time threat detection.

Mobile device management (MDM) and endpoint security solutions complement IAM by securing the devices that employees use to access corporate data. MDM solutions allow IT teams to enforce security policies on mobile devices, such as requiring encryption, enabling remote wipe capabilities, and restricting access to sensitive applications. Endpoint security solutions provide additional protection by detecting malware, preventing unauthorized access, and monitoring device integrity. By integrating MDM and IAM, enterprises can ensure that only compliant devices can access corporate resources, reducing the risk of data breaches.

Enterprise mobility also introduces the challenge of securing cloud applications and services. With the rise of software-as-a-service (SaaS) applications, employees access corporate data from multiple locations and networks. Enterprises use identity federation and single sign-on (SSO) to enable seamless authentication across cloud services while maintaining security. Federated identity allows employees to use their corporate credentials to log into multiple SaaS applications, eliminating the need for separate passwords for each service. By leveraging protocols such as Security Assertion Markup Language (SAML) and OpenID Connect (OIDC), enterprises enable secure and efficient access management across cloud environments.

Zero Trust security models play a crucial role in mobile identity management within enterprises. Unlike traditional perimeter-based security approaches, Zero Trust assumes that no user or device is inherently trusted, regardless of their location. Enterprises implementing Zero Trust enforce continuous authentication, least-privilege access, and contextual risk analysis before granting access to corporate resources. Mobile identity solutions support Zero Trust by verifying user identities, assessing device security posture, and analyzing real-time risk signals. If a login attempt is deemed high-risk, additional authentication factors or access restrictions may be applied to prevent unauthorized access.

Behavioral biometrics and artificial intelligence (AI) enhance mobile identity security by analyzing user behavior and detecting anomalies. Behavioral biometrics assess factors such as typing speed, touch gestures, and navigation patterns to verify identity continuously. AI-driven identity analytics monitor access patterns, flagging suspicious activities such as login attempts from unfamiliar locations or unusual access requests. These technologies enable enterprises to detect and respond to identity threats in real time, reducing the risk of account takeovers and insider threats.

The growing reliance on mobile identity also raises concerns about privacy and regulatory compliance. Enterprises handling sensitive data must comply with regulations such as the General Data Protection Regulation (GDPR), the California Consumer Privacy Act (CCPA), and industry-specific security standards. Mobile identity solutions must ensure that user data is protected through encryption, secure storage, and user consent mechanisms. Additionally, enterprises must implement policies that define how mobile identity data is collected, processed, and retained to meet compliance requirements.

Despite the security benefits of mobile identity, enterprises must address usability challenges to ensure widespread adoption. Employees often resist security measures that introduce friction, such as frequent re-authentication or complex login processes. To balance security and user experience, enterprises implement adaptive authentication, which adjusts authentication requirements based on risk levels. If an employee logs in from a trusted device in a familiar location, authentication may be streamlined, while high-risk login attempts trigger additional verification steps.

As enterprise environments continue to evolve, the role of mobile identity will become even more critical in securing digital interactions. The integration of biometric authentication, AI-driven security, and decentralized identity solutions will further enhance mobile identity management. Enterprises that adopt robust mobile identity strategies will be better equipped to protect their systems, ensure compliance, and provide employees with seamless access to corporate resources.

Identity Lifecycle Management

Managing digital identities is a critical aspect of enterprise security and access control. Identity Lifecycle Management (ILM) refers to the processes and policies governing the creation, maintenance, and eventual deactivation of user identities within an organization. A well-structured ILM framework ensures that employees, contractors, customers, and other users have appropriate access to systems and applications throughout their engagement with an organization while preventing unauthorized access.

The identity lifecycle begins with the onboarding process, where a new user is assigned an identity within the system. In an enterprise environment, this typically occurs when a new employee joins the company or a contractor is granted access to corporate resources. During onboarding, the user is assigned a unique identifier and provisioned with the necessary accounts, roles, and permissions based on their job function. Automated provisioning systems streamline this process by integrating with human resources (HR) databases and directory services, ensuring that new employees receive access to the tools they need without manual intervention.

Once an identity has been created, it must be managed and maintained throughout the user's tenure with the organization. This involves regular updates to access rights based on role changes, department transfers, or project assignments. Role-based access control (RBAC) and attribute-based access control (ABAC) frameworks help organizations enforce security policies by assigning permissions based on predefined criteria. Employees moving to a new department, for example, may require different application access while having their previous permissions revoked to prevent unauthorized access.

Identity governance is an essential component of ILM, ensuring that user access remains appropriate and compliant with security policies. Organizations implement periodic access reviews to verify that employees and contractors still require the permissions assigned to them. These reviews help identify orphaned accounts, which are accounts that remain active after a user has left the organization or changed roles. Failure to properly govern identity lifecycle processes can lead to security vulnerabilities, such as former employees retaining access to sensitive systems or attackers exploiting inactive accounts.

Multi-factor authentication (MFA) and risk-based authentication play a crucial role in maintaining secure identity management. As users interact with enterprise applications and cloud services, continuous authentication mechanisms verify their identity based on contextual factors such as location, device security, and behavioral patterns. If an authentication attempt appears suspicious, additional verification steps may be required before granting access. This dynamic approach enhances security while minimizing user friction.

Identity lifecycle management also involves managing privileged accounts, which have elevated access to critical systems and administrative functions. Privileged Access Management (PAM) solutions help organizations monitor and control the use of privileged credentials, ensuring that only authorized personnel can perform sensitive operations. Temporary privilege escalation is sometimes required for specific tasks, and just-in-time (JIT) access mechanisms grant temporary permissions that automatically expire once the task is completed. This reduces the risk of unauthorized access and insider threats.

Deprovisioning is the final stage of the identity lifecycle and is crucial for maintaining security. When an employee leaves the organization, their access must be revoked immediately to prevent unauthorized entry into corporate systems. Automated deprovisioning processes ensure that all accounts associated with a departing user are disabled or deleted promptly. Additionally, organizations implement account expiration policies for contractors and temporary workers to prevent lingering access beyond their contractual period.

The rise of cloud computing and software-as-a-service (SaaS) applications has introduced additional challenges in ILM. Users often have accounts in multiple cloud platforms, requiring organizations to implement identity federation and single sign-on (SSO) solutions. These technologies enable centralized identity management, allowing users to access multiple applications with a single set of credentials while ensuring that access remains synchronized across all systems.

Compliance with data protection regulations such as the General Data Protection Regulation (GDPR) and the California Consumer Privacy Act (CCPA) requires organizations to implement strong identity lifecycle controls. Regulatory requirements mandate that organizations track and audit identity access activities, ensuring that user data is only accessible to authorized personnel. Implementing audit logs and identity analytics helps organizations detect anomalies, such as unauthorized access attempts or privilege escalations, which may indicate security threats.

Artificial intelligence (AI) and machine learning (ML) are increasingly being integrated into identity lifecycle management solutions to enhance security and automation. AI-driven identity analytics can detect unusual behavior patterns, flagging potential insider threats or compromised accounts. Machine learning algorithms can also automate access request approvals by analyzing historical access patterns and determining whether a request aligns with established policies. These capabilities improve efficiency while reducing administrative overhead for IT teams.

As organizations continue to adopt hybrid work models and cloud-based environments, identity lifecycle management will play a critical role in securing access to corporate resources. A robust ILM strategy not only enhances security but also improves operational efficiency by automating identity-related processes. Organizations must continuously refine their identity lifecycle policies to adapt to evolving cybersecurity threats, regulatory requirements, and technological advancements. By implementing strong ILM frameworks, enterprises can ensure that user access remains secure, compliant, and aligned with business objectives.

Role-Based Access Control (RBAC)

Role-Based Access Control (RBAC) is a widely used security framework that governs how users access resources based on predefined roles within an organization. By assigning permissions to roles rather than individuals, RBAC simplifies access management, enhances security, and ensures that users only have the privileges necessary for their job functions. This approach minimizes the risk of unauthorized access, reduces administrative overhead, and enforces the principle of least privilege, which is a key cybersecurity best practice.

RBAC operates on the principle that access to resources should be granted based on a user's role within an organization rather than on an individual basis. In a typical RBAC implementation, roles are created based on job responsibilities, and permissions are assigned to those roles. Users are then assigned to roles according to their job functions, automatically inheriting the permissions associated with those roles. For example, an organization might define roles such as "HR Manager," "IT Administrator," and "Sales Representative," each with specific access rights to applications, databases, and network resources.

One of the main advantages of RBAC is its ability to enforce the least privilege model, which ensures that users have only the minimum level of access necessary to perform their duties. This reduces the risk of accidental data exposure, insider threats, and privilege escalation attacks. By restricting access based on roles, organizations can prevent unauthorized users from accessing sensitive information or performing actions that could compromise security.

RBAC is particularly beneficial for large organizations with complex IT environments. Managing access on an individual basis in such environments would be impractical and prone to human error. With RBAC, administrators can define role-based policies once and apply them consistently across the organization. If a user changes job roles, their permissions can be updated simply by assigning them to a new role, eliminating the need to manually adjust access rights. This makes onboarding, role changes, and offboarding processes more efficient and secure.

In an RBAC model, roles can be structured in a hierarchical manner, allowing for greater flexibility and scalability. A role hierarchy enables higher-level roles to inherit permissions from lower-level roles. For instance, a "Department Head" role might inherit the permissions of a "Team Lead" role, granting additional privileges while still encompassing the lower-level access rights. This hierarchical approach reduces redundancy in role assignments and simplifies access management.

RBAC also supports separation of duties (SoD), a security principle that prevents conflicts of interest and reduces the risk of fraud or errors. SoD ensures that critical tasks are divided among multiple users, preventing any single individual from having excessive control over sensitive operations. For example, in a financial system, the user responsible for approving transactions should not be the same user responsible for initiating them. RBAC helps enforce SoD policies by restricting permissions based on predefined roles and responsibilities.

Another advantage of RBAC is its ability to streamline compliance with regulatory requirements. Many data protection regulations, such as the General Data Protection Regulation (GDPR), the Health Insurance Portability and Accountability Act (HIPAA), and the Sarbanes-Oxley Act (SOX), require organizations to implement strong access control measures. RBAC helps organizations meet these requirements by providing a structured framework for managing user access, ensuring that only authorized personnel can access sensitive data. Additionally, RBAC facilitates auditability, as access rights are clearly defined and documented, making it easier to track and review user permissions during security audits.

Despite its benefits, implementing RBAC requires careful planning and management to avoid role explosion, a common challenge where an excessive number of roles are created, making the system difficult to manage. Role explosion occurs when too many specific roles are defined to accommodate unique access needs, leading to administrative complexity and potential security gaps. To mitigate this issue, organizations should follow best practices such as role consolidation, defining broad role categories, and using dynamic role assignment based on attributes such as job title, department, or project involvement.

RBAC can be integrated with other identity and access management (IAM) frameworks to enhance security. For example, RBAC can be combined with attribute-based access control (ABAC), which evaluates additional attributes such as location, device type, and access context to determine permissions dynamically. This hybrid approach enhances security by ensuring that access is granted based on both role-based policies and contextual risk factors.

In modern IT environments, RBAC is widely implemented in enterprise systems, cloud platforms, and network security solutions. Cloud service providers such as Amazon Web Services (AWS), Microsoft Azure, and Google Cloud offer RBAC capabilities that allow organizations to define role-based policies for managing access to cloud resources. Similarly, enterprise applications, databases, and operating systems often include built-in RBAC mechanisms to control user permissions and prevent unauthorized actions.

The future of RBAC is evolving with advancements in artificial intelligence (AI) and machine learning (ML). AI-driven access management solutions can analyze user behavior, detect anomalies, and suggest optimized role assignments based on usage patterns. Machine learning algorithms can identify redundant or unnecessary permissions, helping organizations refine their role definitions and improve security. By leveraging AI and automation, organizations can enhance RBAC implementation, reduce administrative effort, and ensure continuous compliance with security policies.

As cyber threats continue to evolve, RBAC remains a fundamental component of access management strategies. Organizations must continuously assess and refine their role structures, enforce least privilege principles, and integrate RBAC with modern identity management technologies to maintain a secure and efficient access control framework. A well-implemented RBAC system not only enhances security but also improves operational efficiency, ensuring that users have the right level of access while minimizing risk.

Attribute-Based Access Control (ABAC)

Attribute-Based Access Control (ABAC) is an advanced access control model that determines permissions based on a combination of attributes related to the user, resource, environment, and actions being performed. Unlike Role-Based Access Control (RBAC), which relies solely on predefined roles, ABAC provides a more dynamic and context-aware approach to authorization, making it ideal for modern security environments where access decisions must be flexible and adaptable.

ABAC operates by evaluating a set of attributes before granting or denying access to a resource. Attributes can include user-specific details such as job title, department, security clearance level, or even behavioral patterns. Resource attributes define properties related to the data or system being accessed, such as classification level, ownership, or data sensitivity. Environmental attributes consider external factors like time of day, location, device type, network security posture, and regulatory requirements. Finally, action attributes define the type of operation being requested, such as read, write, edit, or delete. By analyzing these attributes collectively, ABAC ensures that access control decisions are made based on real-time contextual information rather than static role assignments.

One of the primary advantages of ABAC is its flexibility and scalability. Traditional RBAC models require administrators to create and manage multiple roles, which can lead to role explosion as organizations grow and access requirements become more complex. ABAC eliminates this issue by using attributes instead of predefined roles, allowing organizations to define fine-grained access policies without the need for excessive role management. This makes ABAC particularly beneficial for large enterprises, government agencies, and cloud-based environments where users require varying levels of access based on different conditions.

For example, in an enterprise setting, an employee working in the finance department may be granted access to financial reports, but only if they are accessing the system from a corporate network during business hours. If the same employee attempts to access the data from an untrusted device or outside regular working hours, ABAC policies could restrict access or require additional authentication. This level of control allows organizations to enforce security policies dynamically, reducing the risk of unauthorized access while maintaining operational efficiency.

ABAC is also highly effective in compliance-driven industries such as healthcare, banking, and government, where access to sensitive data must adhere to strict regulations. For instance, in a hospital setting, a doctor may have permission to view patient records, but only for patients under their care. If an unauthorized individual attempts to access the same records, ABAC policies can automatically deny access based on attributes such as job role, patient assignment, or location. This granular approach to access control helps organizations comply with regulations like the Health Insurance Portability and Accountability Act (HIPAA) and the General Data Protection Regulation (GDPR) by ensuring that only authorized users can access specific data under defined conditions.

One of the challenges of implementing ABAC is defining and managing attribute-based policies effectively. Unlike RBAC, which assigns roles with fixed permissions, ABAC requires organizations to develop complex policies that account for multiple attributes and contextual factors. This can lead to increased administrative overhead, particularly in organizations that lack a structured approach to defining access control policies. To address this challenge, enterprises often use policy management frameworks such as the eXtensible Access Control Markup Language (XACML), which provides a standardized way to define, enforce, and evaluate ABAC policies.

Another key consideration in ABAC implementation is the need for real-time attribute evaluation. Since ABAC policies rely on dynamic attributes such as location and device security status, access control decisions must be made instantly based on current conditions. This requires integration with identity and access management (IAM) systems, security information and event management (SIEM) solutions, and real-time analytics tools that can provide up-to-date attribute data. Machine learning and artificial intelligence are increasingly being integrated into ABAC systems to analyze user behavior and detect anomalies that may indicate potential security threats.

ABAC is particularly well-suited for cloud environments and hybrid IT architectures, where users frequently access resources from different devices and locations. Cloud service providers such as Amazon Web Services (AWS), Microsoft Azure, and Google Cloud offer ABAC-based access control mechanisms that allow organizations to define policies based on attributes such as user identity, resource classification, and network security posture. This level of control ensures that sensitive cloud data remains protected while allowing authorized users to access resources efficiently.

The integration of ABAC with Zero Trust security models further enhances its effectiveness in preventing unauthorized access. Zero Trust operates on the principle that no user or device should be inherently trusted, requiring continuous authentication and authorization based on contextual attributes. By leveraging ABAC, Zero Trust architectures can enforce dynamic access controls that adapt to changing security conditions, ensuring that only legitimate users with the appropriate attributes can access critical systems and data.

Despite its benefits, transitioning to an ABAC model requires careful planning and policy definition. Organizations must first identify key attributes that will be used to enforce access control decisions, ensuring that these attributes are accurate, relevant, and up to date. Additionally, policy management must be automated to reduce administrative complexity and ensure consistency across different systems and applications. Continuous monitoring and auditing are also essential to verify that ABAC policies are functioning as intended and to detect any unauthorized access attempts.

As organizations continue to adopt cloud-based applications, mobile work environments, and hybrid IT infrastructures, the need for dynamic and context-aware access control solutions is becoming more critical. ABAC provides a scalable, flexible, and security-enhancing approach to access management by evaluating real-time attributes and enforcing fine-grained policies. By implementing ABAC effectively, enterprises can strengthen security, improve regulatory compliance, and provide users with seamless yet controlled access to digital resources.

Decentralized Identity and Blockchain

The traditional approach to digital identity relies on centralized systems where user data is stored and managed by a single authority, such as a government agency, a financial institution, or a social media platform. While this model has been effective for many years, it presents significant security, privacy, and control challenges. Centralized identity management systems are prone to data breaches, identity theft, and unauthorized access. As users become more aware of the risks associated with sharing personal information with third-party entities, the need for a more secure and user-centric identity framework has emerged. Decentralized identity, powered by blockchain technology, offers a transformative approach that shifts control from centralized authorities to individuals, enabling greater privacy, security, and autonomy over personal data.

Decentralized identity is based on the principle that users should have complete ownership and control over their digital identities. Instead of relying on a single entity to store and verify identity credentials, decentralized identity systems distribute identity management across a network of nodes, making it more secure and resistant to fraud. This model eliminates the need for intermediaries, allowing users to authenticate themselves directly with service providers while maintaining full control over their personal information. Decentralized identity is often built on blockchain or distributed ledger technology (DLT), which provides a secure and tamper-resistant way to store and verify identity data.

Blockchain technology plays a critical role in decentralized identity by enabling trustless and verifiable transactions without the need for a central authority. In a blockchain-based identity system, identity credentials are issued as verifiable credentials (VCs) and stored in a user's digital wallet. These credentials can be presented to service providers when authentication is required, without exposing unnecessary personal details. Unlike traditional identity verification methods, where service providers must contact a central database to validate a user's identity, blockchain allows for direct verification through cryptographic proofs, reducing reliance on third-party authorities.

Self-sovereign identity (SSI) is a key concept within decentralized identity, emphasizing user ownership and control of personal identity data. In an SSI model, users store their identity credentials in a digital wallet on their mobile device or secure hardware, rather than on a centralized server. When a service provider requests identity verification, the user can share only the necessary information without revealing additional personal data. For example, instead of providing a full government-issued ID to verify age, an SSI system can generate a cryptographic proof that confirms the user is over a certain age without disclosing their birthdate or other sensitive details. This selective disclosure capability enhances privacy and security, reducing the risk of identity fraud.

Decentralized Identifiers (DIDs) are another fundamental component of decentralized identity. DIDs are unique, cryptographically verifiable identifiers that users can generate and control without relying on a central registry. Unlike traditional identifiers such as email addresses or social security numbers, which are assigned by external entities, DIDs enable users to create multiple identities for different purposes while maintaining privacy. A DID can be associated with various verifiable credentials, allowing users to authenticate themselves in different contexts without revealing unnecessary information. The World Wide Web Consortium (W3C) has developed standards for DIDs, ensuring interoperability across decentralized identity systems.

One of the most significant benefits of decentralized identity and blockchain is enhanced security. Traditional identity systems store vast amounts of sensitive data in centralized databases, making them attractive targets for cyberattacks. Data breaches in centralized identity systems can expose millions of user records, leading to identity theft and financial fraud. In contrast, decentralized identity systems do not rely on a single point of failure. Since identity credentials are stored securely on user-controlled devices and verified through blockchain, the risk of large-scale data breaches is significantly reduced. Furthermore, blockchain's immutability ensures that identity records cannot be tampered with or altered without authorization.

Another advantage of decentralized identity is improved user privacy. In centralized identity models, service providers collect and store user data, often sharing it with third parties for advertising or analytics purposes. This widespread data collection raises concerns about user tracking, profiling, and surveillance. With decentralized identity, users decide which information to share and with whom, minimizing data exposure and protecting their privacy. This approach aligns with global data protection regulations such as the General Data Protection Regulation (GDPR) and the California Consumer Privacy Act (CCPA), which emphasize user control over personal data.

Decentralized identity and blockchain are particularly beneficial in scenarios where identity verification is challenging, such as in financial inclusion and digital identity for refugees. Many individuals in developing regions lack access to formal identification documents, making it difficult to access banking, healthcare, and government services. Blockchain-based identity systems can provide a secure and portable identity solution that enables individuals to prove their identity without relying on traditional documentation. By using verifiable credentials, individuals can establish trust with service providers while maintaining control over their identity data.

Despite its advantages, decentralized identity and blockchain face several challenges that must be addressed before widespread adoption can occur. One of the primary challenges is interoperability between different decentralized identity solutions. Various organizations and consortia are developing blockchain-based identity frameworks, but without standardized protocols, cross-platform compatibility remains a concern. Efforts by organizations such as the Decentralized Identity Foundation (DIF) and the W3C are helping to establish common standards for decentralized identity, ensuring that different systems can work together seamlessly.

Another challenge is user adoption and ease of use. While decentralized identity empowers users with greater control over their personal information, managing cryptographic keys and digital wallets can be complex for non-technical users. To drive mainstream adoption, decentralized identity solutions must offer user-friendly interfaces and seamless authentication experiences comparable to traditional identity systems. Integrating decentralized identity with existing authentication methods, such as biometrics and passwordless authentication, can help bridge the gap between security and usability.

Regulatory considerations also play a critical role in the adoption of decentralized identity. Governments and regulatory bodies must define legal frameworks for decentralized identity to ensure compliance with existing identity verification standards. Additionally, organizations must address concerns related to the legal recognition of verifiable credentials and the accountability of identity issuers. Collaborative efforts between governments, private sector entities, and technology providers will be essential in establishing decentralized identity as a trusted and legally recognized authentication method.

As digital interactions continue to expand, decentralized identity and blockchain have the potential to redefine how identity is managed and verified online. By shifting control from centralized entities to individuals, this approach enhances security, privacy, and user autonomy. While challenges remain, ongoing advancements in blockchain technology, cryptographic security, and decentralized identity standards are paving the way for a more secure and user-centric identity ecosystem. Organizations and governments must work together to ensure that decentralized identity solutions are scalable, interoperable, and accessible to all users, ultimately enabling a more secure and privacy-respecting digital future.

Self-Sovereign Identity (SSI)

The concept of identity has evolved significantly in the digital age, moving from traditional paper-based credentials to centralized digital identity systems. While these systems provide convenience, they also come with security risks, privacy concerns, and dependency on third-party authorities. Self-Sovereign Identity (SSI) is a revolutionary approach to digital identity that gives individuals full control over their identity credentials without relying on a central authority. By leveraging decentralized technologies such as blockchain, cryptographic security, and verifiable credentials, SSI enables users to manage, share, and verify their identities in a secure and privacy-preserving manner.

Self-Sovereign Identity is built on the principle that individuals should own and control their identity data, rather than having it managed by governments, corporations, or other entities. Traditional identity models require users to store their personal information in centralized databases, exposing them to data breaches and unauthorized access. SSI eliminates this risk by allowing users to store their identity credentials in a secure digital wallet, where they can selectively share information with service providers as needed. This decentralized approach enhances security, reduces reliance on intermediaries, and protects user privacy.

One of the key components of SSI is the use of decentralized identifiers (DIDs). A DID is a unique, cryptographically verifiable identifier that is not controlled by any single authority. Unlike email addresses, social security numbers, or government-issued IDs, which are assigned by external entities, DIDs allow individuals to create their own identifiers that are independent of any organization. These identifiers can be used to authenticate with different services while maintaining privacy and security. The World Wide Web Consortium (W3C) has developed standards for DIDs, ensuring interoperability across different SSI systems.

Another critical element of SSI is verifiable credentials (VCs). Verifiable credentials are digitally signed identity documents that prove certain attributes about an individual. These credentials can be issued by trusted organizations, such as governments, universities, or banks, and stored in a user's digital wallet. When a user needs to verify their identity, they can present a cryptographic proof of their verifiable credential without revealing unnecessary personal details. For example, a person applying for a job may need to prove they have a university degree, but instead of sharing a full transcript, they can provide a cryptographic proof that verifies their degree without exposing additional information.

SSI enhances privacy through selective disclosure, which allows users to share only the necessary information required for a transaction. Traditional identity verification methods often require users to provide excessive personal data, increasing the risk of identity theft. With SSI, individuals can present zero-knowledge proofs, a cryptographic method that confirms the validity of certain claims without revealing the underlying data. For example, instead of showing a driver's license to prove they are over 18, a person can use a zero-knowledge proof that simply confirms their age without disclosing their birthdate or other personal details.

Blockchain technology plays a fundamental role in enabling SSI by providing a secure and tamper-proof mechanism for verifying identities. Unlike traditional identity systems that rely on centralized databases, SSI uses distributed ledger technology (DLT) to ensure that identity credentials cannot be altered or forged. When an entity issues a verifiable credential, a cryptographic proof of that credential is recorded on a blockchain. This allows verifiers to check the authenticity of a credential without needing to contact the issuer directly. Since blockchain data is immutable, it provides a reliable and trustless way to validate identity claims.

Self-Sovereign Identity also addresses the problem of identity portability. In traditional identity systems, users must repeatedly register and verify their identities with different service providers, leading to fragmented digital identities. SSI enables users to have a single portable identity that can be used across multiple platforms without the need to reauthenticate every time. This reduces friction in online interactions and enhances user convenience while maintaining security.

One of the major applications of SSI is in financial services, where identity verification is crucial for compliance with regulations such as Know Your Customer (KYC) and Anti-Money Laundering (AML). Banks and financial institutions can use SSI to streamline identity verification, reducing onboarding times and eliminating the need for repeated document submissions. Since verifiable credentials are issued by trusted authorities and can be instantly validated, financial institutions can authenticate users more efficiently while reducing fraud risks.

SSI also has significant implications for government and public services. Governments can issue digital identity credentials that citizens store in their wallets and use for various services, such as voting, tax filing, and healthcare access. Estonia, for example, has implemented a digital identity system that allows citizens to access government services securely and efficiently. By adopting SSI, governments can improve identity verification while empowering citizens with greater control over their personal information.

Another important use case of SSI is identity inclusion for individuals who lack formal identification. Millions of people worldwide do not have access to government-issued IDs, making it difficult for them to participate in financial systems, healthcare, and education. SSI provides a decentralized identity solution that allows individuals to build and verify their identity using credentials from trusted entities, such as NGOs, local communities, or educational institutions. This helps bridge the gap for individuals without traditional forms of identification, enabling greater access to essential services.

Despite its advantages, SSI faces several challenges that must be addressed for widespread adoption. Interoperability is a key concern, as different organizations and governments develop SSI frameworks using varying technologies and standards. Ensuring compatibility between different SSI systems is essential for seamless identity verification across platforms. Additionally, user adoption and education are critical, as managing decentralized identities and cryptographic keys requires a shift in mindset for individuals accustomed to traditional identity models. Simplifying the user experience and providing intuitive digital wallet applications can help drive adoption.

Regulatory and legal considerations also play a role in the implementation of SSI. While decentralized identity aligns with privacy regulations such as GDPR and CCPA, governments must establish legal frameworks to recognize and support self-sovereign identity. Questions surrounding identity verification, liability, and fraud prevention need to be addressed to ensure that SSI is both secure and legally compliant.

The development of SSI is being driven by global initiatives and organizations, including the Decentralized Identity Foundation (DIF), the World Wide Web Consortium (W3C), and the Sovrin Foundation. These groups are working to create standards and frameworks that will facilitate the widespread adoption of decentralized identity solutions. As the technology matures, SSI is expected to play a significant role in transforming digital identity management by enhancing security, privacy, and user autonomy.

By shifting control of identity data from centralized authorities to individuals, SSI represents a fundamental shift in how digital identities are managed. With its ability to enhance privacy, reduce fraud, and provide seamless authentication across services, Self-Sovereign Identity has the potential to redefine trust and security in the digital world.

Mobile Identity and Digital Wallets

As digital interactions become more integrated into daily life, the need for secure and convenient identity management solutions has grown significantly. Mobile identity, which allows users to authenticate and verify their identities through mobile devices, has become a crucial component of modern digital ecosystems. One of the key enablers of mobile identity is the digital wallet, a secure application that stores identity credentials, payment methods, and other personal information. Digital wallets not only streamline authentication and access control but also enhance security by reducing reliance on passwords and physical identity documents.

A digital wallet, also known as an e-wallet, is a mobile application that allows users to store and manage digital versions of identity documents, payment cards, loyalty programs, and other credentials. These wallets are typically protected by biometric authentication, such as fingerprint scanning or facial recognition, ensuring that only authorized users can access stored credentials. Unlike traditional physical wallets, which can be lost or stolen, digital wallets offer enhanced security features such as encryption, tokenization, and remote device management, reducing the risk of identity theft and fraud.

One of the primary use cases of mobile identity and digital wallets is in financial transactions. Digital payment systems such as Apple Pay, Google Pay, and Samsung Pay allow users to make secure purchases using their smartphones without needing to enter credit card details manually. These payment systems leverage near-field communication (NFC) technology to facilitate contactless transactions while ensuring security through tokenization. Instead of transmitting actual credit card numbers, digital wallets generate unique transaction tokens, preventing attackers from intercepting sensitive financial information.

Beyond financial transactions, digital wallets are increasingly being used for identity verification and authentication. Governments, businesses, and educational institutions are adopting digital identity solutions that allow individuals to store and present verifiable credentials in their digital wallets. For example, mobile driver's licenses (mDLs) are being implemented in several regions, allowing users to present their digital ID on their smartphones instead of carrying a physical card. Similarly, universities are issuing digital student IDs, enabling students to access campus facilities, attend events, and verify their status with a simple tap of their mobile device.

The integration of mobile identity with digital wallets has also revolutionized travel and border security. Digital passports and mobile boarding passes allow travelers to store their travel documents on their smartphones, reducing the need for physical paperwork. Some airports and border control agencies have implemented biometric authentication systems that enable travelers to verify their identity using facial recognition, streamlining security checks and reducing wait times. By leveraging digital wallets for identity verification, travel authorities can enhance security while providing a seamless experience for passengers.

Health credentials are another area where mobile identity and digital wallets have become increasingly important. The COVID-19 pandemic accelerated the adoption of digital health passes, which allow individuals to store and present vaccination records, test results, and medical certificates on their mobile devices. Digital health credentials use verifiable credentials and cryptographic signatures to ensure authenticity, preventing fraud and forgery. By integrating health credentials into digital wallets, individuals can securely share their medical information with healthcare providers, employers, and travel authorities without compromising privacy.

One of the key benefits of mobile identity and digital wallets is their ability to support self-sovereign identity (SSI). SSI allows individuals to control and manage their digital identity without relying on centralized authorities. Instead of storing identity data in government or corporate databases, SSI-enabled digital wallets store verifiable credentials directly on users' devices, giving them full control over how and when their identity is shared. This decentralized approach enhances privacy, reduces the risk of data breaches, and aligns with emerging data protection regulations such as the General Data Protection Regulation (GDPR).

Security remains a critical consideration in mobile identity and digital wallet implementations. While digital wallets provide strong authentication mechanisms, they are also attractive targets for cybercriminals. To mitigate security risks, mobile wallets implement encryption, biometric authentication, and hardware-backed security measures such as Secure Enclave (Apple) or Trusted Execution Environment (Android). Additionally, digital wallets often incorporate multi-factor authentication (MFA) and risk-based authentication to prevent unauthorized access.

Interoperability is another challenge in the adoption of mobile identity and digital wallets. Various platforms and standards exist for digital identity verification, including Decentralized Identifiers (DIDs), Verifiable Credentials (VCs), and OpenID Connect. Ensuring compatibility between different wallet providers, identity issuers, and service providers is essential for creating a seamless digital identity ecosystem. Industry organizations such as the World Wide Web Consortium (W3C) and the Decentralized Identity Foundation (DIF) are working to establish common standards that facilitate cross-platform interoperability and trust.

The future of mobile identity and digital wallets is expected to include further advancements in biometric authentication, artificial intelligence (AI), and blockchain technology. AI-powered identity verification can enhance fraud detection by analyzing behavioral patterns and detecting anomalies in authentication attempts. Blockchain-based identity solutions can provide decentralized identity verification, eliminating the need for intermediaries while ensuring the integrity of identity credentials. As these technologies continue to evolve, mobile identity and digital wallets will play an even greater role in enabling secure and frictionless digital interactions.

With increasing reliance on digital services, the adoption of mobile identity and digital wallets will continue to grow across various industries. Governments, financial institutions, healthcare providers, and enterprises are all recognizing the benefits of mobile identity solutions for enhancing security, reducing fraud, and improving user convenience. By leveraging digital wallets, users can consolidate their identity credentials, payments, and access control mechanisms into a single, secure platform, paving the way for a more streamlined and privacy-focused digital identity experience.

Mobile ID in Government and Public Services

Governments around the world are embracing digital transformation to improve the efficiency, security, and accessibility of public services. One of the most significant advancements in this digital era is the adoption of Mobile ID, a digital identity solution that enables citizens to authenticate themselves using their mobile devices. Mobile ID provides a secure and convenient way for individuals to access government services, sign documents, and verify their identities without the need for physical identification cards. By integrating mobile identity solutions into public services, governments can enhance service delivery, reduce fraud, and improve citizen engagement.

Mobile ID allows individuals to store their government-issued identification, such as passports, national IDs, and driver's licenses, in a secure digital format on their smartphones. Instead of carrying physical documents, citizens can authenticate themselves using their mobile devices, which typically rely on biometric authentication methods such as fingerprint recognition, facial scanning, or iris recognition. This approach not only enhances security but also streamlines identity verification processes across various government services.

One of the most common applications of Mobile ID in government is electronic identity (eID) programs. Many countries have implemented eID systems that enable citizens to access public services online, eliminating the need for in-person visits to government offices. Estonia, for example, is a global leader in digital identity, offering a comprehensive eID system that allows citizens to file taxes, vote in elections, and sign legal documents electronically. By adopting Mobile ID, governments can expand the capabilities of traditional eID programs, enabling citizens to authenticate themselves remotely through their smartphones.

Mobile ID also plays a crucial role in digital voting systems. As governments explore ways to increase voter participation and enhance election security, mobile-based authentication is emerging as a viable solution. With Mobile ID, citizens can securely verify their identity and cast their votes from their smartphones, reducing the risk of voter fraud and improving accessibility for remote or disabled voters. While digital voting presents challenges such as cybersecurity risks and ensuring the integrity of election results, Mobile ID provides a strong foundation for secure and transparent electronic voting systems.

Another important application of Mobile ID is in public healthcare services. Citizens can use their Mobile ID to securely access their medical records, schedule appointments, and verify prescriptions. Digital health credentials, such as vaccination records and electronic health cards, can be stored in mobile wallets, allowing individuals to present their health information when required without carrying physical documents. Governments can also integrate Mobile ID with telemedicine services, enabling remote consultations with healthcare providers while ensuring secure patient authentication.

Law enforcement agencies and border control authorities are also leveraging Mobile ID for identity verification. Digital passports and mobile-based border authentication systems allow travelers to use their smartphones for immigration checks, reducing wait times and improving security at airports and border crossings. Some countries have introduced digital driver's licenses that can be presented during traffic stops, eliminating the need for physical cards. These mobile-based identity solutions enhance security by incorporating biometric verification and cryptographic security measures that prevent document forgery.

Social welfare programs can also benefit from Mobile ID integration. Governments provide various social services, including unemployment benefits, pension distributions, and food assistance programs. By using Mobile ID, citizens can securely access these benefits without the need for paper-based verification processes. Digital identity solutions help reduce fraud and ensure that only eligible individuals receive government assistance. Additionally, Mobile ID can be used to streamline identity verification for refugees and displaced persons, allowing them to access humanitarian aid and essential services even if they lack physical identification documents.

Taxation and financial services are other key areas where Mobile ID is making an impact. Governments are increasingly adopting digital identity solutions for secure tax filing and financial transactions. Mobile ID allows citizens to log into tax portals, submit declarations, and make payments securely without needing complex passwords or physical documents. By integrating Mobile ID with banking services, governments can facilitate secure online banking, digital payments, and financial aid distribution, reducing the risk of identity fraud and enhancing financial inclusion.

Mobile ID implementation requires strong security measures to protect citizens' personal information. Governments must ensure that Mobile ID systems are resistant to cyber threats such as phishing attacks, identity theft, and unauthorized access. Encryption, biometric authentication, and decentralized identity frameworks help secure digital identities and protect sensitive data from misuse. Additionally, regulations such as the General Data Protection Regulation (GDPR) and other data privacy laws must be followed to ensure that citizens have control over how their identity information is used and shared.

Interoperability is a crucial factor in the success of Mobile ID in government and public services. Many countries are working towards developing global standards for digital identity verification, allowing citizens to use their Mobile ID across borders. The European Union's eIDAS (Electronic Identification, Authentication, and Trust Services) regulation is an example of a framework that enables secure cross-border identity verification within EU member states. By ensuring interoperability between different Mobile ID systems, governments can create a seamless experience for citizens who need to verify their identity across multiple jurisdictions.

Despite its numerous benefits, Mobile ID adoption comes with challenges, including digital divide concerns and accessibility issues. Not all citizens have access to smartphones or the necessary digital literacy to use Mobile ID effectively. Governments must ensure that alternative identity verification methods are available for individuals who may not be able to use mobile-based authentication. Additionally, public awareness campaigns and educational initiatives are essential to encourage widespread adoption of Mobile ID and inform citizens about its benefits and security features.

The future of Mobile ID in government and public services is expected to evolve with advancements in biometric authentication, artificial intelligence (AI), and blockchain technology. AI-powered fraud detection can enhance identity verification by analyzing behavioral patterns and detecting anomalies. Blockchain-based identity solutions can provide decentralized authentication methods that reduce reliance on central authorities while ensuring data integrity and security. As these technologies continue to mature, governments will have more tools to enhance the efficiency, security, and accessibility of public services through Mobile ID solutions.

By leveraging Mobile ID, governments can modernize identity verification, streamline service delivery, and improve citizen engagement. From eGovernment portals to healthcare services, border control, and financial transactions, Mobile ID provides a secure and efficient way for citizens to interact with public services. As adoption continues to grow, Mobile ID will play a critical role in shaping the future of digital identity in governance and beyond.

Mobile Identity for Banking and Finance

The financial sector has undergone a significant transformation with the rise of digital banking and mobile payment solutions. As consumers increasingly rely on smartphones for banking transactions, securing digital identities has become a top priority for financial institutions. Mobile identity plays a critical role in enabling secure access to banking services, preventing fraud, and improving customer experience. By leveraging biometric authentication, multi-factor authentication (MFA), and decentralized identity frameworks, banks and financial service providers can enhance security while ensuring seamless interactions for their customers.

Mobile identity in banking refers to the use of mobile devices as a means of authenticating users and verifying their identities during financial transactions. Traditional banking authentication methods, such as passwords and PINs, are increasingly being replaced by more secure mobile-based authentication mechanisms. Biometric authentication, including fingerprint recognition, facial recognition, and voice authentication, allows customers to access their accounts with a simple scan or voice command, reducing reliance on easily compromised credentials.

One of the primary benefits of mobile identity in banking is enhanced security. The financial sector is a prime target for cybercriminals, with fraudsters frequently using phishing attacks, account takeovers, and credential stuffing techniques to gain unauthorized access to user accounts. Mobile identity solutions mitigate these risks by implementing strong authentication measures. Multi-factor authentication (MFA) is commonly used in mobile banking apps, requiring users to verify their identity through a combination of factors such as a password, a mobile device, and biometric data. By adding additional layers of security, MFA makes it significantly harder for attackers to compromise customer accounts.

Mobile identity also plays a key role in Know Your Customer (KYC) and Anti-Money Laundering (AML) compliance. Banks and financial institutions are required to verify the identities of their customers before providing services to prevent fraud, money laundering, and terrorist financing. Mobile-based identity verification streamlines the KYC process by allowing customers to submit digital copies of their identification documents, such as passports or driver's licenses, through their smartphones. Advanced identity verification technologies, including optical character recognition (OCR) and artificial intelligence (AI)-powered facial matching, ensure the authenticity of submitted documents while reducing the need for in-person verification.

Digital wallets and mobile payment systems further enhance the role of mobile identity in finance. Services such as Apple Pay, Google Pay, and Samsung Pay allow users to store their credit and debit card information securely on their smartphones. These mobile payment platforms use tokenization to protect sensitive card data by replacing it with unique, encrypted tokens during transactions. This method significantly reduces the risk of card fraud, as the actual card details are never shared with merchants. Additionally, biometric authentication is often required before completing transactions, adding an extra layer of security.

Financial institutions are also exploring the use of decentralized identity solutions to improve customer privacy and security. Decentralized identity frameworks allow users to control their identity credentials without relying on a central authority. Instead of storing personal data on a bank's servers, users can store their identity information in a secure digital wallet on their mobile device. When identity verification is required, they can share only the necessary information using verifiable credentials and cryptographic proofs. This approach reduces the risk of identity theft and data breaches, as sensitive information is not stored in a central database that could be compromised.

Another key application of mobile identity in banking is fraud detection and risk-based authentication. Many financial institutions use AI-driven identity analytics to monitor customer behavior and detect anomalies in real time. If a customer suddenly logs in from an unfamiliar location or device, the system may require additional authentication, such as a biometric scan or a push notification approval on their mobile device. These adaptive security measures help prevent unauthorized transactions while minimizing inconvenience for legitimate users.

Mobile identity is also transforming peer-to-peer (P2P) payments and remittances. Services such as PayPal, Venmo, and Zelle enable users to send and receive money using their mobile phones. To prevent fraud, these platforms rely on mobile identity verification, linking user accounts to verified phone numbers, email addresses, and biometric authentication. Additionally, digital identity verification helps prevent unauthorized account creation and ensures compliance with financial regulations.

Banks and financial service providers are also leveraging blockchain technology to enhance mobile identity security. Blockchain-based identity verification offers a tamper-proof and decentralized way to authenticate users while reducing reliance on third-party identity providers. By using blockchain, financial institutions can create a trusted and verifiable identity ecosystem that enhances security, reduces fraud, and simplifies cross-border transactions. Some initiatives are exploring the use of self-sovereign identity (SSI), allowing individuals to own and manage their financial identity independently, without intermediaries.

While mobile identity offers numerous benefits for banking and finance, its implementation comes with challenges. One major concern is ensuring accessibility for all users, particularly those without smartphones or reliable internet access. Financial institutions must ensure that alternative authentication methods are available for individuals who may not have access to mobile devices. Additionally, regulatory compliance remains a challenge, as financial authorities impose strict guidelines on data privacy and identity verification. Banks must ensure that their mobile identity solutions comply with regulations such as the General Data Protection Regulation (GDPR) and the Payment Services Directive 2 (PSD2).

As financial institutions continue to adopt mobile identity solutions, they must strike a balance between security and user convenience. While stronger authentication measures enhance security, they should not create excessive friction for customers. Biometric authentication, AI-driven fraud detection, and risk-based authentication help achieve this balance by providing seamless yet secure access to banking services. By leveraging mobile identity, the financial sector can improve security, streamline compliance processes, and offer a more user-friendly banking experience.

Mobile Identity in Healthcare

The healthcare industry is increasingly adopting digital solutions to improve patient care, enhance security, and streamline administrative processes. Mobile identity plays a crucial role in this transformation by enabling secure access to medical records, telehealth services, and electronic prescriptions. As hospitals, clinics, and healthcare providers transition to digital identity solutions, mobile identity ensures that patient data remains protected while allowing healthcare professionals to deliver efficient and personalized care.

Mobile identity in healthcare refers to the use of mobile devices for identity verification, authentication, and access control within medical environments. Traditionally, healthcare organizations have relied on physical ID cards, usernames and passwords, and in-person verification to authenticate patients and medical staff. However, these methods can be inefficient, prone to security risks, and cumbersome for both patients and providers. By leveraging mobile identity solutions, healthcare organizations can replace outdated authentication methods with biometric authentication, mobile-based digital IDs, and secure mobile applications.

One of the most significant applications of mobile identity in healthcare is electronic health records (EHR) access. EHR systems store patients' medical histories, test results, treatment plans, and other sensitive information that must be securely accessed by authorized healthcare professionals. Mobile identity solutions enhance EHR security by enabling multi-factor authentication (MFA) and biometric login methods, such as fingerprint or facial recognition. This ensures that only verified medical personnel can access patient records while minimizing the risk of unauthorized access or data breaches.

Telemedicine has also seen rapid growth, with mobile identity playing a key role in verifying patient and provider identities during virtual consultations. As telehealth services expand, ensuring secure authentication is critical to prevent identity fraud and unauthorized access to medical information. Mobile identity solutions allow patients to authenticate themselves using their smartphones before joining a virtual appointment, while healthcare providers can verify their credentials to ensure they are licensed professionals. Secure mobile identity verification prevents medical fraud and ensures compliance with healthcare regulations such as the Health Insurance Portability and Accountability Act (HIPAA).

Another critical aspect of mobile identity in healthcare is e-prescriptions and pharmacy access. Many healthcare systems now allow doctors to issue electronic prescriptions that patients can fill at pharmacies without the need for physical paper prescriptions. Mobile identity verification ensures that only authorized doctors can prescribe medication and that patients can securely retrieve their prescriptions. Digital wallets integrated with mobile identity solutions allow patients to store and present digital prescriptions, reducing the risk of prescription fraud and medication errors.

Patient identity verification is a major challenge in healthcare, especially in emergency situations where immediate access to medical records is necessary. Mobile identity solutions enable secure patient identification by linking patients' medical records to their verified digital identity. Instead of relying on manual patient identification methods, which can be slow and prone to errors, hospitals can use mobile authentication systems that allow patients to verify their identity instantly via their smartphones. This not only improves patient safety but also reduces administrative burdens on healthcare providers.

Wearable devices and mobile health (mHealth) apps are becoming increasingly popular for monitoring chronic conditions, fitness levels, and general health. Mobile identity ensures that the data collected from these devices remains secure and accessible only to authorized users. Patients can grant access to their health data for specific healthcare providers, ensuring that their personal medical information remains private. Mobile identity also facilitates secure data sharing between different healthcare providers, improving coordination of care for patients with complex medical needs.

Medical staff authentication is another area where mobile identity provides significant benefits. Doctors, nurses, and other healthcare professionals require secure access to medical systems, treatment plans, and administrative tools. Traditional authentication methods, such as passwords, are inefficient and can create security vulnerabilities. Mobile identity solutions enable single sign-on (SSO) authentication, allowing medical staff to access multiple healthcare applications with a single, secure login. Biometric authentication further enhances security by ensuring that only authorized personnel can access critical healthcare systems.

Healthcare fraud prevention is another key benefit of mobile identity. Medical identity theft and fraudulent billing claims cost the healthcare industry billions of dollars each year. By implementing strong mobile identity verification methods, such as biometric authentication and secure digital credentials, healthcare providers can prevent unauthorized access to medical services and reduce fraudulent insurance claims. Mobile identity also helps ensure that government healthcare benefits, such as Medicare and Medicaid, are only accessed by eligible individuals.

Regulatory compliance is a critical consideration for healthcare organizations adopting mobile identity solutions. Regulations such as HIPAA in the United States, GDPR in Europe, and other data protection laws mandate strict security measures for handling patient data. Mobile identity solutions must comply with these regulations by ensuring encryption, data minimization, and user consent mechanisms. Secure identity management frameworks, including decentralized identity and blockchain-based verification, offer additional layers of security and transparency in patient data management.

Interoperability is a key challenge in mobile identity adoption within healthcare. Different healthcare providers, insurance companies, and government agencies often use separate identity verification systems, making it difficult for patients to access their medical records seamlessly. Efforts to standardize mobile identity frameworks, such as the Fast Healthcare Interoperability Resources (FHIR) standard, aim to improve data sharing across healthcare systems. By integrating mobile identity solutions with standardized identity management frameworks, healthcare organizations can enhance data interoperability while maintaining security and privacy.

Despite the benefits of mobile identity in healthcare, there are challenges to widespread adoption. Digital inclusion and accessibility must be considered to ensure that all patients, including elderly individuals and those in rural or underserved areas, can access mobile identity solutions. Healthcare providers must offer alternative authentication methods, such as voice recognition or physical authentication tokens, for individuals who may not have smartphones or digital literacy skills.

The future of mobile identity in healthcare will continue to evolve with advancements in artificial intelligence (AI), machine learning, and blockchain technology. AI-powered identity verification can detect anomalies and prevent identity fraud, while blockchain-based identity solutions offer decentralized, tamper-proof authentication. Self-sovereign identity (SSI) models will further empower patients by allowing them to own and control their medical data without relying on centralized databases.

Mobile identity is transforming the healthcare industry by enabling secure, seamless, and efficient identity verification. From electronic health record access and telemedicine authentication to prescription security and medical staff verification, mobile identity ensures that healthcare services remain secure while improving patient experience and data privacy. As the adoption of mobile identity continues to grow, healthcare organizations must prioritize security, compliance, and accessibility to fully realize the benefits of digital identity in patient care.

Mobile Identity for E-Commerce

The rise of mobile commerce has transformed the way consumers shop online, with mobile devices now accounting for a significant portion of e-commerce transactions. As shoppers increasingly rely on smartphones and tablets for browsing, purchasing, and payment processing, ensuring secure and seamless authentication is essential. Mobile identity plays a critical role in e-commerce by enabling secure logins, fraud prevention, personalized shopping experiences, and fast transactions. By leveraging mobile authentication methods such as biometrics, multi-factor authentication (MFA), and digital wallets, e-commerce platforms can enhance security while improving user experience.

Mobile identity in e-commerce refers to the use of mobile devices as a primary method for authenticating users and verifying their identities during online transactions. Traditional authentication methods, such as usernames and passwords, are often vulnerable to security threats such as credential theft, phishing, and brute force attacks. Mobile identity solutions provide stronger security by integrating advanced authentication mechanisms, such as fingerprint scanning, facial recognition, and one-time passwords (OTPs). These methods not only improve security but also reduce friction for customers, enabling a smoother shopping experience.

One of the most significant benefits of mobile identity in e-commerce is the ability to streamline the login process. Many online retailers now support passwordless authentication, allowing users to sign in using biometric authentication or mobile-based authentication tokens instead of traditional passwords. This approach reduces password fatigue, minimizes the risk of credential stuffing attacks, and improves overall security. Single sign-on (SSO) solutions further enhance the user experience by enabling customers to log in once and access multiple e-commerce platforms without re-entering their credentials.

Fraud prevention is a major concern in e-commerce, as cybercriminals frequently target online retailers with fraudulent transactions, identity theft, and account takeovers. Mobile identity verification helps mitigate these risks by implementing strong authentication measures and risk-based security checks. For example, if a customer attempts to log in from an unfamiliar device or location, the system can trigger additional verification steps, such as requiring biometric authentication or an OTP sent to their mobile device. This adaptive security approach prevents unauthorized access while ensuring legitimate customers can shop without unnecessary disruptions.

Mobile identity also plays a key role in seamless checkout experiences. Digital wallets, such as Apple Pay, Google Pay, and Samsung Pay, enable customers to complete transactions with a single tap, eliminating the need to manually enter payment details. These wallets use tokenization to replace credit card numbers with unique transaction tokens, preventing exposure of sensitive financial information. By integrating mobile identity with digital wallets, e-commerce platforms can reduce checkout abandonment rates and increase conversion rates by providing a fast and secure payment experience.

Another important application of mobile identity in e-commerce is identity verification for high-value transactions. Some purchases, such as luxury goods, electronics, or online ticketing, require additional security checks to prevent fraud. Mobile identity solutions allow retailers to verify customer identities in real-time using government-issued digital IDs, biometric verification, or mobile-based identity documents. By incorporating mobile identity verification into the purchasing process, e-commerce platforms can minimize fraudulent transactions while maintaining a frictionless shopping experience for legitimate buyers.

Personalization is another area where mobile identity enhances e-commerce. When users authenticate through their mobile identity, retailers can leverage their verified information to provide a more personalized shopping experience. Mobile identity enables retailers to tailor product recommendations, loyalty programs, and targeted promotions based on customers' preferences and purchase history. By integrating mobile identity with AI-driven analytics, e-commerce platforms can offer personalized discounts, exclusive offers, and a seamless shopping journey that enhances customer engagement.

Loyalty programs and customer retention strategies are also strengthened through mobile identity. Many retailers offer digital loyalty cards that can be stored in a mobile wallet, eliminating the need for physical cards. Customers can earn and redeem rewards simply by authenticating with their mobile identity, creating a frictionless and engaging shopping experience. Additionally, mobile identity can be used to verify customers participating in exclusive membership programs, ensuring that only eligible users receive premium benefits and discounts.

Mobile identity also enhances customer support and account recovery. Traditional account recovery methods, such as email-based password resets, can be exploited by attackers through phishing and social engineering attacks. Mobile identity solutions provide a more secure alternative by allowing users to verify their identity through biometric authentication or SMS-based authentication links. This approach reduces the risk of account takeovers and ensures that customers can regain access to their accounts quickly and securely.

Regulatory compliance is another important consideration for e-commerce businesses implementing mobile identity solutions. Many countries have introduced data protection laws, such as the General Data Protection Regulation (GDPR) and the California Consumer Privacy Act (CCPA), which require companies to implement strong security measures for handling customer data. Mobile identity solutions help retailers comply with these regulations by ensuring that customer authentication processes are secure, encrypted, and privacy-focused. Additionally, the Payment Services Directive 2 (PSD2) in Europe mandates the use of strong customer authentication (SCA) for online payments, requiring multi-factor authentication methods such as biometrics or OTPs to verify transactions.

Despite its advantages, the adoption of mobile identity in e-commerce also comes with challenges. User education and adoption remain critical factors, as some customers may be unfamiliar with mobile identity authentication methods or hesitant to use biometric authentication for online transactions. Retailers must invest in clear communication strategies, educating users on the security benefits of mobile identity and providing easy-to-use authentication options.

Another challenge is ensuring cross-platform compatibility and interoperability. Customers use a variety of devices, operating systems, and browsers to shop online, requiring e-commerce platforms to support multiple authentication standards. Implementing OpenID Connect, FIDO2, and WebAuthn ensures that mobile identity solutions work seamlessly across different devices while maintaining security.

Looking ahead, the future of mobile identity in e-commerce will be shaped by emerging technologies such as decentralized identity and blockchain. Decentralized identity solutions allow customers to store and control their identity credentials on their mobile devices, reducing reliance on centralized databases that can be targeted by hackers. Blockchain-based identity verification provides an immutable and tamper-proof authentication system, further enhancing security for online transactions.

Artificial intelligence (AI) and machine learning will also play a crucial role in mobile identity verification by enabling behavioral biometrics and real-time fraud detection. AI-driven authentication systems can analyze user behavior, such as typing patterns, touchscreen interactions, and location data, to detect anomalies and prevent unauthorized transactions. These advancements will further strengthen security while maintaining a frictionless shopping experience for consumers.

By integrating mobile identity solutions, e-commerce businesses can enhance security, improve customer experience, and reduce fraud. With biometric authentication, digital wallets, and AI-driven identity verification, online retailers can create a seamless and secure shopping environment that meets the evolving needs of mobile consumers. As mobile commerce continues to grow, adopting robust mobile identity strategies will be essential for building trust and ensuring long-term success in the digital marketplace.

Mobile Device Management (MDM) and Identity

As organizations increasingly rely on mobile devices for business operations, securing these devices and managing user identities have become critical priorities. Mobile Device Management (MDM) is a technology that enables IT administrators to control, secure, and enforce policies on mobile devices used within an enterprise. When combined with identity and access management (IAM), MDM ensures that only authorized users with compliant devices can access corporate networks, applications, and sensitive data. This integration strengthens security while enabling organizations to maintain productivity in an increasingly mobile workforce.

MDM solutions allow businesses to manage various aspects of mobile devices, including security policies, application control, and remote management capabilities. These solutions are particularly important in environments where employees use their personal devices for work under Bring Your Own Device (BYOD) policies. Without proper device management, unauthorized access, data breaches, and malware infections become significant risks. By enforcing identity-based access controls through MDM, organizations can ensure that only verified users and compliant devices can connect to corporate resources.

One of the primary functions of MDM is device authentication and enrollment. Before a mobile device can access an organization's network or applications, it must be registered with the MDM system. During the enrollment process, the device is assigned a unique identifier, and security policies are applied based on the user's role and access privileges. Identity management systems work alongside MDM by ensuring that only authenticated users can enroll their devices. This prevents unauthorized devices from gaining access to corporate resources, reducing the risk of security breaches.

Multi-Factor Authentication (MFA) and Conditional Access are essential components of integrating MDM with identity management. Many organizations implement MFA to verify user identity before granting access to corporate applications. This typically involves a combination of passwords, biometrics, and authentication codes sent to a trusted device. However, MFA alone is not enough to secure mobile environments. Conditional access policies enhance security by evaluating factors such as device compliance, location, network security, and user behavior before allowing access. For example, if a user attempts to log in from an unmanaged device or an unfamiliar location, additional authentication steps may be required, or access may be denied altogether.

MDM solutions also play a crucial role in data encryption and secure access control. Organizations must ensure that sensitive business data stored on mobile devices is encrypted to prevent unauthorized access in case of device loss or theft. MDM platforms allow administrators to enforce encryption policies, ensuring that all corporate data remains protected. In addition, MDM can restrict access to corporate applications based on identity policies. For instance, an employee may be allowed to access email and collaboration tools on a managed device but restricted from downloading or copying sensitive files to an unmanaged personal device.

Another key feature of MDM is remote wipe and device lock capabilities. In the event that a mobile device is lost, stolen, or compromised, IT administrators can remotely lock or erase the device to prevent unauthorized access to corporate data. This is especially important in industries with strict regulatory requirements, such as finance, healthcare, and government. By integrating MDM with identity management, organizations can automate these security responses based on identity verification and risk analysis. For example, if an employee's credentials are compromised, their associated devices can be flagged for remote wiping to prevent further security threats.

Application management and identity governance are also essential components of MDM. Organizations often deploy enterprise applications that require strict access controls and identity verification. MDM solutions enable IT teams to manage app permissions, restrict app installations, and ensure that only authorized users can access corporate applications. By integrating MDM with IAM, businesses can implement Single Sign-On (SSO), allowing employees to authenticate once and gain access to multiple corporate applications without needing to re-enter credentials. This approach not only improves security but also enhances user experience by reducing login friction.

The Zero Trust security model further strengthens the integration of MDM and identity management. Zero Trust operates on the principle of "never trust, always verify," requiring continuous authentication and authorization for all users and devices accessing corporate networks. By combining MDM with Zero Trust principles, organizations can enforce identity verification at every access point, ensuring that devices meet security compliance standards before connecting to sensitive resources. This reduces the risk of insider threats and advanced persistent threats (APTs) that target mobile endpoints.

Regulatory compliance and data protection laws necessitate strong mobile identity management practices. Regulations such as the General Data Protection Regulation (GDPR), the California Consumer Privacy Act (CCPA), and industry-specific standards like HIPAA and PCI DSS require organizations to implement strict access controls and data protection measures. MDM solutions help businesses comply with these regulations by enforcing identity-based policies, securing data in transit and at rest, and providing audit trails for identity verification and device access.

Despite its advantages, implementing MDM and identity management presents challenges. Organizations must balance security with user privacy, especially in BYOD environments where employees use personal devices for work. Overly restrictive policies can lead to frustration and resistance, while insufficient security controls can expose businesses to cyber threats. To address this, businesses should adopt a user-centric approach to MDM, providing employees with clear policies, privacy assurances, and secure alternatives for accessing corporate resources.

Another challenge is device fragmentation and compatibility. With a wide range of mobile devices, operating systems, and security configurations in use, ensuring uniform security policies across all devices can be complex. Organizations must select MDM solutions that support multiple platforms, including iOS, Android, and Windows, while ensuring seamless integration with identity providers and cloud-based IAM solutions.

The future of MDM and identity management is expected to evolve with advancements in artificial intelligence (AI) and machine learning. AI-powered identity analytics can enhance mobile security by detecting behavioral anomalies, such as unusual login patterns or unauthorized data access. Machine learning algorithms can adapt security policies dynamically based on real-time risk assessments, improving threat detection and response times. Additionally, decentralized identity solutions using blockchain technology could further enhance mobile identity security by reducing reliance on centralized authentication providers and minimizing data exposure risks.

As organizations continue to embrace mobile workforces and cloud-based services, MDM and identity management will remain essential for securing enterprise data and user access. By integrating strong authentication measures, enforcing conditional access policies, and leveraging Zero Trust security frameworks, businesses can mitigate risks while enabling a seamless and productive mobile experience for employees. Organizations that invest in robust MDM and identity solutions will be better equipped to navigate the evolving cybersecurity landscape and protect their digital assets from emerging threats.

Identity and Access Management (IAM) in Mobile Ecosystems

The rapid expansion of mobile technology has transformed the way users interact with digital services, requiring organizations to implement robust security measures to protect sensitive data. Identity and Access Management (IAM) plays a critical role in securing mobile ecosystems by ensuring that only authorized users can access applications, services, and corporate resources. As mobile devices become central to authentication and digital identity, IAM solutions must adapt to provide seamless security while maintaining user convenience.

IAM in mobile ecosystems encompasses a range of identity verification, authentication, and access control mechanisms designed to protect mobile applications and enterprise networks. Unlike traditional IAM systems, which primarily focused on desktop environments, mobile IAM must account for additional security challenges such as device variability, network vulnerabilities, and user mobility. Organizations must implement IAM frameworks that can manage access across multiple devices, applications, and cloud services while ensuring compliance with security policies and regulatory requirements.

One of the key components of IAM in mobile environments is user authentication. Traditional password-based authentication methods are no longer sufficient due to their susceptibility to phishing attacks, credential theft, and brute force attempts. Instead, organizations are adopting more secure authentication mechanisms such as biometric authentication, multi-factor authentication (MFA), and passwordless authentication. Biometric authentication, including fingerprint recognition, facial scanning, and voice authentication, provides a seamless and secure method for verifying user identities on mobile devices. MFA further enhances security by requiring users to verify their identity using multiple authentication factors, reducing the risk of unauthorized access.

Single Sign-On (SSO) is another important IAM feature in mobile ecosystems. SSO allows users to authenticate once and gain access to multiple applications without having to re-enter credentials. This simplifies the user experience while enhancing security by reducing the reliance on passwords. Many enterprises implement SSO solutions based on identity federation protocols such as Security Assertion Markup Language (SAML) and OpenID Connect (OIDC), enabling seamless authentication across mobile applications, cloud platforms, and enterprise networks.

IAM solutions in mobile ecosystems must also incorporate risk-based authentication (RBA) to dynamically adjust authentication requirements based on contextual risk factors. RBA analyzes factors such as user location, device type, network security, and behavioral patterns to determine the risk level of an authentication attempt. For example, if a user logs in from an unfamiliar device or an untrusted network, the system may prompt additional authentication steps, such as requiring biometric verification or a one-time passcode. This adaptive security approach ensures that authentication remains strong while minimizing friction for legitimate users.

Device identity and security posture play a crucial role in mobile IAM strategies. Unlike traditional computing environments, mobile ecosystems involve a wide range of devices, including smartphones, tablets, and wearable devices, each with different security capabilities. IAM solutions must verify not only the user's identity but also the security posture of the device attempting to access corporate resources. Mobile Device Management (MDM) and endpoint security solutions help enforce compliance by ensuring that only trusted and secure devices can connect to enterprise applications. Organizations can implement policies that restrict access from jailbroken or rooted devices, enforce device encryption, and mandate security updates to reduce vulnerabilities.

Role-based access control (RBAC) and attribute-based access control (ABAC) are essential for managing user permissions in mobile environments. RBAC assigns access rights based on predefined roles within an organization, ensuring that employees, contractors, and partners can only access the information necessary for their job functions. ABAC enhances this approach by considering additional attributes such as device location, user behavior, and security posture to dynamically adjust access permissions. These access control models help organizations enforce the principle of least privilege, reducing the risk of data breaches and insider threats.

The Zero Trust security model further strengthens IAM in mobile ecosystems by requiring continuous authentication and strict access controls. Unlike traditional perimeter-based security models, which assume that users inside the network are trustworthy, Zero Trust operates on the principle of "never trust, always verify." In a Zero Trust framework, every access request is authenticated, authorized, and continuously monitored based on real-time security assessments. IAM solutions integrate with Zero Trust architectures by verifying user identity, assessing device compliance, and enforcing least-privilege access policies.

IAM in mobile environments must also ensure secure API access and integration with cloud services. Many mobile applications rely on cloud-based APIs to retrieve and process data, making API security a critical aspect of mobile IAM. OAuth 2.0 and OpenID Connect are widely used protocols that enable secure authentication and authorization for mobile applications. By implementing these standards, organizations can ensure that mobile apps and services authenticate users securely while maintaining control over API access.

Identity federation and decentralized identity solutions are emerging trends in IAM that enhance privacy and security in mobile ecosystems. Identity federation enables users to authenticate with one organization and access services provided by other trusted entities without creating multiple accounts. This is particularly useful in enterprise environments where employees need to access third-party applications. Decentralized identity solutions, powered by blockchain technology, further enhance IAM by allowing users to manage their digital identity independently, without relying on centralized identity providers. Self-sovereign identity (SSI) models enable users to store verifiable credentials on their mobile devices and selectively share identity information with service providers, reducing the risk of identity theft and data breaches.

Regulatory compliance and data privacy are key considerations for IAM in mobile ecosystems. Many countries have implemented stringent data protection laws, such as the General Data Protection Regulation (GDPR) in Europe and the California Consumer Privacy Act (CCPA) in the United States. IAM solutions must comply with these regulations by implementing data minimization practices, encryption, and user consent mechanisms. Organizations must ensure that mobile IAM frameworks provide audit logs and reporting capabilities to demonstrate compliance with regulatory requirements.

Despite the benefits of IAM in mobile ecosystems, challenges remain in ensuring usability and seamless authentication. Users expect fast and frictionless access to mobile applications, and overly complex authentication processes can lead to frustration and abandonment. Organizations must balance security and usability by implementing authentication mechanisms that are both strong and user-friendly. Context-aware authentication, behavioral biometrics, and AI-driven identity analytics can help streamline authentication while maintaining high security standards.

As mobile technology continues to evolve, IAM solutions must adapt to new threats, user expectations, and regulatory requirements. The integration of AI, machine learning, and blockchain-based identity verification will further enhance mobile IAM by improving threat detection, automating risk assessments, and providing users with greater control over their digital identities. By implementing comprehensive IAM frameworks, organizations can protect sensitive data, prevent unauthorized access, and provide secure, seamless authentication experiences in an increasingly mobile-driven world.

Risk-Based Authentication (RBA)

Risk-Based Authentication (RBA) is an advanced security mechanism that dynamically adjusts authentication requirements based on the risk level associated with a login attempt. Unlike traditional authentication methods that apply the same security measures to all users, RBA evaluates contextual factors such as device information, location, behavior patterns, and network security before determining the level of authentication required. This adaptive approach enhances security while minimizing friction for legitimate users, striking a balance between user convenience and strong identity protection.

The fundamental principle behind RBA is to assess the likelihood of fraudulent access and apply appropriate authentication measures accordingly. If a login attempt is deemed low risk, the user may be granted access with minimal authentication steps, such as entering a username and password. However, if the system detects an anomaly, such as an unusual login location, a new device, or an abnormal access pattern, additional authentication steps—such as multi-factor authentication (MFA), biometric verification, or a one-time passcode (OTP)—may be triggered.

One of the key factors analyzed in RBA is user behavior and login patterns. Many organizations employ behavioral analytics to establish baseline login patterns for users, including preferred devices, typical locations, and access times. When a user logs in from a familiar environment, the authentication process remains seamless. However, if a deviation from normal behavior is detected—such as an attempt to access an account from a different country or an unrecognized device—the system flags the login attempt as high risk and prompts additional security measures.

Device intelligence is another critical component of RBA. The authentication system evaluates whether the device used for login is recognized and has been previously associated with the user's account. If a known device is used, the system may grant access with minimal authentication. However, if a login attempt is made from an unknown or suspicious device, the system may require additional verification, such as biometric authentication or an SMS-based OTP. Device fingerprinting techniques, which analyze factors like browser version, operating system, and IP address, help determine whether the login attempt is legitimate.

Geolocation and network security analysis play a significant role in RBA assessments. If a user frequently logs in from a specific geographic region, an authentication request from that area may be considered low risk. However, if a login attempt originates from an unusual location or a known high-risk region associated with fraudulent activity, the system may require enhanced verification. Additionally, RBA examines the security of the network being used. For example, a login from a secure corporate network may be treated as low risk, whereas an attempt from a public Wi-Fi network or an anonymized VPN could trigger stricter authentication measures.

One of the biggest advantages of RBA is its ability to prevent credential-based attacks. Traditional username and password authentication is highly vulnerable to credential stuffing, phishing, and brute force attacks. RBA reduces the effectiveness of these attacks by requiring additional authentication steps for suspicious login attempts, making it significantly harder for attackers to gain unauthorized access even if they possess stolen credentials. By implementing RBA, organizations can significantly reduce account takeover risks and improve overall security posture.

RBA is widely used in banking, finance, and e-commerce, where security is paramount. Many online banking platforms implement RBA to protect customer accounts from unauthorized transactions. If a user logs in from an unrecognized device or attempts to transfer a large sum of money to a new recipient, additional verification steps may be required to confirm the user's identity. Similarly, e-commerce platforms use RBA to secure online purchases by assessing transaction risks and prompting verification methods when unusual buying patterns are detected.

In addition to enhancing security, RBA also improves user experience and frictionless authentication. One of the biggest drawbacks of traditional MFA is that it requires users to authenticate every time they log in, even when accessing their accounts from trusted environments. RBA solves this issue by dynamically adjusting authentication requirements based on risk. Users logging in from familiar devices and locations can access their accounts without additional authentication steps, while high-risk attempts undergo more stringent verification. This improves convenience while maintaining security.

Artificial intelligence (AI) and machine learning (ML) are increasingly being integrated into RBA systems to enhance threat detection and risk analysis. AI-driven RBA continuously learns from user behavior, identifying patterns and anomalies more accurately over time. Machine learning algorithms analyze vast amounts of authentication data to distinguish between legitimate and suspicious login attempts, enabling real-time decision-making. These AI-powered systems can also detect bot-driven attacks, automated credential stuffing, and social engineering tactics, adapting authentication requirements to counter evolving threats.

Despite its advantages, implementing RBA requires careful planning and privacy considerations. Since RBA collects and analyzes user data such as location, device information, and behavioral patterns, organizations must ensure compliance with data protection regulations such as the General Data Protection Regulation (GDPR) and the California Consumer Privacy Act (CCPA). Users must be informed about the data being collected, and organizations should implement encryption and anonymization techniques to protect sensitive information.

Another challenge of RBA implementation is balancing security and usability. Overly strict authentication policies can lead to false positives, frustrating legitimate users by requiring unnecessary verification steps. Conversely, lenient policies may fail to detect sophisticated attacks. To address this, organizations should continuously refine their RBA models based on real-world authentication data, adjusting risk thresholds to optimize security while minimizing user inconvenience.

Looking ahead, the future of RBA will likely involve biometric authentication, behavioral biometrics, and decentralized identity solutions. Biometric authentication methods, such as facial recognition and fingerprint scanning, provide a strong layer of security that enhances RBA decision-making. Behavioral biometrics, which analyze factors such as keystroke dynamics, mouse movements, and touchscreen interactions, can further improve identity verification by detecting anomalies in real time. Decentralized identity frameworks, powered by blockchain technology, may also play a role in RBA by enabling verifiable credentials that users control independently, reducing reliance on centralized identity providers.

Organizations adopting RBA must ensure seamless integration with existing Identity and Access Management (IAM) frameworks and authentication protocols such as OAuth 2.0, OpenID Connect (OIDC), and Security Assertion Markup Language (SAML). By integrating RBA with IAM, organizations can enforce least privilege access policies, ensuring that users only receive access to the resources necessary for their roles.

With cyber threats becoming more sophisticated, RBA is emerging as a critical security layer for protecting digital identities. By dynamically adjusting authentication requirements based on real-time risk assessments, RBA significantly enhances security while reducing authentication friction for legitimate users. As organizations continue to adopt cloud-based services, mobile identity solutions, and digital banking platforms, implementing robust RBA strategies will be essential for mitigating threats and safeguarding sensitive information in an increasingly digital world.

Continuous Authentication

As digital security threats evolve, traditional authentication methods based on one-time verification at login are no longer sufficient to protect sensitive data and user accounts. Continuous authentication is an advanced security approach that monitors and verifies user identity throughout an active session, rather than only at the initial login attempt. By continuously evaluating behavioral patterns, device signals, and environmental factors, continuous authentication enhances security while reducing reliance on static credentials. This method is particularly useful in mobile environments, cloud-based applications, and high-security industries where unauthorized access can lead to severe consequences.

Continuous authentication operates on the principle of ongoing identity verification, ensuring that the user interacting with a device or application remains the legitimate account holder throughout the session. Unlike traditional authentication, which grants access after a single verification step, continuous authentication dynamically evaluates multiple signals in real time to detect anomalies. If suspicious activity is detected, the system can prompt additional authentication steps, restrict access, or terminate the session to prevent unauthorized activity.

One of the key components of continuous authentication is behavioral biometrics, which analyzes unique user behaviors to establish identity. Behavioral biometrics includes factors such as typing patterns, touchscreen gestures, mouse movements, and navigation habits. Since these behaviors are difficult to replicate, behavioral biometrics provides a reliable method of continuous verification. For example, if a banking app detects a sudden change in typing rhythm or touchscreen interaction, it may prompt the user for reauthentication, such as biometric verification or a security challenge.

Device intelligence and contextual signals also play a crucial role in continuous authentication. The system evaluates whether the device being used remains consistent with the user's typical behavior. If a session is initiated on a trusted smartphone but later accessed from an unrecognized device, the system may enforce additional verification steps. Contextual signals such as geolocation, network status, and IP address further enhance security by identifying potential anomalies. If a user logs in from a known location but later attempts to perform sensitive actions from a different country within minutes, continuous authentication mechanisms can flag the session as suspicious and require identity confirmation.

Artificial intelligence (AI) and machine learning (ML) enhance continuous authentication by learning user behavior over time and detecting deviations from normal patterns. AI-driven models analyze vast amounts of authentication data to differentiate between legitimate and fraudulent access attempts. By recognizing subtle behavior changes, AI-powered continuous authentication systems can proactively prevent unauthorized access without disrupting user experience. For example, if an employee working remotely exhibits a sudden and unusual shift in behavior, the system may trigger an authentication challenge before allowing further access.

One of the biggest advantages of continuous authentication is its ability to reduce reliance on passwords. Since authentication occurs in the background based on real-time behavioral and contextual analysis, users do not need to repeatedly enter passwords or authentication codes. This improves both security and convenience, reducing the risks associated with password-based authentication methods such as phishing, credential stuffing, and brute force attacks.

Continuous authentication is particularly valuable in high-security industries such as finance, healthcare, and government services, where unauthorized access can have serious implications. Banks and financial institutions use continuous authentication to protect online transactions, ensuring that only the legitimate account owner can initiate payments or access sensitive financial data. Similarly, healthcare organizations implement continuous authentication to safeguard electronic health records (EHRs) and prevent unauthorized modifications to patient information.

Zero Trust security frameworks align closely with continuous authentication principles by enforcing strict verification at every access attempt. In a Zero Trust model, no user or device is inherently trusted, and access permissions are continuously reassessed based on dynamic risk factors. Continuous authentication supports Zero Trust by providing real-time monitoring and adaptive security controls, ensuring that access is granted only when the user's identity remains verified throughout the session.

Another key application of continuous authentication is fraud prevention and identity protection. Cybercriminals often exploit session hijacking techniques, where they take control of an authenticated session without triggering login security checks. Continuous authentication mitigates this risk by continuously verifying user identity and detecting session takeovers in real time. If an attacker gains unauthorized access but exhibits behavior inconsistent with the legitimate user, the system can revoke access, alert security teams, or enforce additional verification measures.

Multi-factor authentication (MFA) and continuous authentication can work together to provide a layered security approach. While MFA secures the initial login process, continuous authentication ensures ongoing security throughout the session. If a risk is detected, the system can prompt a secondary authentication factor, such as a fingerprint scan or an SMS-based OTP, before allowing further actions. This dynamic approach enhances protection while minimizing user disruption.

Despite its security benefits, implementing continuous authentication comes with challenges. Balancing security and user experience is a critical consideration, as overly aggressive authentication prompts can frustrate users and disrupt workflows. To address this, organizations must fine-tune authentication policies to minimize unnecessary security challenges while maintaining strong protection. By leveraging AI-driven analytics and adaptive authentication models, businesses can create frictionless authentication experiences that do not interfere with legitimate user activity.

Privacy concerns also play a role in continuous authentication adoption. Since this method involves continuous monitoring of user behavior and contextual data, organizations must ensure compliance with data protection regulations such as the General Data Protection Regulation (GDPR) and the California Consumer Privacy Act (CCPA). Users should be informed about how their data is collected, stored, and used, and security teams must implement strong encryption and anonymization techniques to protect sensitive authentication data.

The future of continuous authentication will likely involve advancements in biometric verification, decentralized identity, and behavioral AI models. More organizations are expected to adopt biometric authentication as a core component of continuous identity verification, leveraging facial recognition, voice authentication, and iris scanning. Additionally, decentralized identity solutions, where users control their authentication credentials without relying on centralized databases, could further enhance security and privacy in continuous authentication frameworks.

As cyber threats continue to evolve, organizations must prioritize security solutions that provide both strong protection and seamless user experiences. Continuous authentication offers a proactive security model that adapts to real-time risks, ensuring that only legitimate users can maintain access to sensitive data and digital services. By integrating AI-driven analytics, behavioral biometrics, and contextual authentication, organizations can build robust, adaptive security frameworks that protect against unauthorized access while maintaining user-friendly authentication processes.

Identity Threats and Vulnerabilities

Digital identity has become a fundamental component of modern online interactions, enabling users to access services, perform transactions, and authenticate themselves across various platforms. However, as identity management systems evolve, so do the threats and vulnerabilities associated with them. Cybercriminals continuously develop sophisticated techniques to exploit weaknesses in identity security, leading to data breaches, financial fraud, and unauthorized access. Understanding the most common identity threats and vulnerabilities is essential for organizations and individuals to protect their digital identities effectively.

One of the most prevalent identity threats is phishing, a social engineering attack that tricks users into revealing their credentials by impersonating a legitimate entity. Cybercriminals send fraudulent emails, text messages, or phone calls that appear to be from a trusted organization, such as a bank or a well-known service provider. These messages often contain urgent requests, such as verifying an account or updating payment details, leading users to fake login pages designed to steal their credentials. Phishing remains one of the most effective attack methods because it exploits human psychology rather than technical vulnerabilities.

Another significant identity threat is credential stuffing, a cyberattack in which hackers use stolen username-password combinations from previous data breaches to gain unauthorized access to user accounts. Since many users reuse passwords across multiple services, credential stuffing can be highly effective, allowing attackers to take over accounts with minimal effort. Automated scripts and botnets enable cybercriminals to test thousands of credentials quickly, increasing the likelihood of success. Organizations can mitigate this risk by implementing multi-factor authentication (MFA) and encouraging users to adopt strong, unique passwords for each account.

Brute force attacks are another method used to compromise digital identities. In a brute force attack, an attacker systematically tries different password combinations until they find the correct one. This can be done using automated tools that generate millions of password attempts per second. While this attack is less effective against strong passwords, weak or commonly used passwords make it easier for attackers to gain access. Organizations can counter brute force attacks by enforcing password complexity policies, implementing account lockout mechanisms, and using risk-based authentication.

A growing concern in identity security is session hijacking, where an attacker intercepts an active user session to gain unauthorized access to an account or service. This is often achieved through man-in-the-middle (MitM) attacks, where the attacker eavesdrops on or manipulates communication between the user and the server. Public Wi-Fi networks, especially unsecured ones, are common targets for MitM attacks, as attackers can intercept session cookies or authentication tokens transmitted over the network. To mitigate session hijacking risks, users should enable encrypted connections (HTTPS), use VPNs when accessing sensitive accounts from public networks, and rely on security measures such as token expiration and re-authentication.

Another critical vulnerability is identity theft, where attackers steal personal information to impersonate individuals, open fraudulent accounts, or commit financial fraud. Identity theft often occurs through data breaches, where attackers gain access to databases containing sensitive personal information, such as social security numbers, addresses, and banking details. Once this information is obtained, cybercriminals can use it to apply for credit cards, take out loans, or even assume complete control over a victim's digital identity. Identity theft protection services and credit monitoring can help detect unauthorized activities, but organizations must prioritize data encryption, access controls, and breach detection to prevent identity theft from occurring in the first place.

Account takeover (ATO) attacks are a significant threat to both individuals and businesses. In an ATO attack, cybercriminals gain unauthorized access to user accounts, often by exploiting weak passwords, phishing tactics, or leaked credentials from data breaches. Once inside an account, attackers may change passwords, steal sensitive data, make fraudulent transactions, or use the compromised account for further attacks. Companies can reduce the risk of ATO attacks by enforcing strong authentication policies, monitoring for unusual login behaviors, and providing users with secure account recovery options.

A sophisticated identity-related attack is synthetic identity fraud, in which criminals create entirely new identities by combining real and fake information. Unlike traditional identity theft, synthetic identity fraud does not rely solely on stolen personal data but instead builds new personas using fabricated details, such as false addresses, phone numbers, and social security numbers. These fake identities are used to apply for credit, take out loans, and conduct fraudulent transactions, often without detection. Financial institutions and government agencies must enhance identity verification processes by leveraging biometric authentication, AI-powered fraud detection, and cross-referencing identity data with trusted sources.

Insider threats pose another challenge in identity security. Employees, contractors, or business partners with legitimate access to corporate systems may misuse their privileges for financial gain, espionage, or personal grievances. Insider threats can be intentional, such as stealing company data, or unintentional, such as an employee falling victim to a phishing attack and unknowingly exposing sensitive credentials. Organizations must implement strict access controls, monitor user activity, and employ behavioral analytics to detect suspicious actions that may indicate an insider threat.

Biometric spoofing is a relatively new identity attack that targets biometric authentication systems. Attackers use advanced techniques such as fake fingerprints, facial recognition bypass methods, and deepfake technology to trick biometric security systems. While biometric authentication is generally more secure than passwords, it is not foolproof. To counter biometric spoofing, organizations should implement liveness detection mechanisms, multi-factor authentication, and continuous authentication methods to ensure ongoing identity verification.

A persistent issue in identity security is poor password hygiene among users. Many people continue to use weak passwords, reuse passwords across multiple sites, or fail to update passwords regularly. Even with password managers and security awareness campaigns, weak passwords remain a major vulnerability. Organizations must enforce strong password policies, educate users on secure authentication practices, and encourage passwordless authentication methods such as biometric authentication and cryptographic keys.

Emerging identity threats include deepfake technology and AI-driven impersonation attacks. Deepfake-generated videos and voice recordings can be used to impersonate individuals in real-time, posing a serious challenge to identity verification systems. Attackers can manipulate biometric authentication methods or trick identity verification processes in social engineering attacks. The rise of AI-driven threats requires organizations to integrate advanced fraud detection systems, behavioral biometrics, and AI-based identity verification methods to combat emerging risks.

Addressing identity threats and vulnerabilities requires a multi-layered security approach, combining strong authentication, encryption, behavioral analytics, and continuous monitoring. Organizations must adopt a proactive security strategy that includes real-time threat detection, user education, and regulatory compliance to minimize identity-related risks. By staying ahead of evolving cyber threats and implementing robust identity protection measures, businesses and individuals can strengthen their digital identities against malicious attacks.

Mobile Phishing and Identity Theft

The rise of mobile technology has brought unprecedented convenience to digital interactions, allowing users to access banking, social media, and business applications from anywhere. However, this shift has also created new opportunities for cybercriminals to exploit users through mobile phishing and identity theft. Unlike traditional cyberattacks that target desktop environments, mobile phishing takes advantage of smaller screens, limited security awareness, and the growing reliance on mobile communication channels, making it a major threat to digital identity security.

Mobile phishing refers to social engineering attacks that attempt to deceive users into revealing sensitive information, such as login credentials, credit card details, or personal data. Attackers often use email, text messages (SMS), messaging apps, and even malicious mobile applications to lure victims into clicking on fraudulent links or downloading malware. The mobile ecosystem presents unique vulnerabilities that make phishing attacks more effective, including users' tendency to act quickly on notifications, the difficulty of verifying website URLs on small screens, and the lack of robust phishing protections on mobile browsers compared to desktop counterparts.

One of the most common forms of mobile phishing is SMS phishing (smishing), where attackers send text messages impersonating legitimate entities such as banks, government agencies, or service providers. These messages often contain urgent alerts, such as suspicious account activity or package delivery notifications, prompting users to click on a malicious link. Once the user clicks the link, they are typically redirected to a fake website that mimics the legitimate service, where they are tricked into entering their login credentials. Smishing is particularly effective because users tend to trust SMS messages more than emails, making them less skeptical of fraudulent texts.

Another prevalent attack method is phishing via messaging apps such as WhatsApp, Facebook Messenger, and Telegram. Attackers exploit these platforms to spread malicious links, often disguising them as promotional offers, urgent security warnings, or social invitations. Unlike emails, messages on these apps often come from contacts within a user's network, making them appear more trustworthy. Cybercriminals also use compromised accounts to send phishing messages, making it harder for victims to detect fraud.

Email-based phishing remains a significant threat to mobile users, especially as more people access email accounts on their smartphones. Mobile email clients often display only the sender's name, making it easier for attackers to spoof trusted contacts or brands. Since users frequently check emails on the go, they may not take the time to scrutinize message details before clicking on links or downloading attachments. Attackers exploit this behavior to deploy fraudulent emails containing fake login portals or malicious files designed to steal credentials or install spyware on mobile devices.

One of the most dangerous aspects of mobile phishing is its connection to identity theft. Once attackers obtain personal information through phishing schemes, they can use it for various forms of fraud, including financial fraud, account takeovers, and identity impersonation. Stolen credentials are often sold on the dark web, where cybercriminals use them to access bank accounts, apply for credit cards, or engage in fraudulent transactions. Victims of mobile phishing attacks may not immediately realize their information has been compromised, giving attackers time to exploit stolen identities before detection.

Another evolving mobile phishing threat is voice phishing (vishing), where attackers impersonate legitimate organizations over the phone to extract personal information from victims. Using caller ID spoofing, cybercriminals can make it appear as though their calls originate from banks, government agencies, or tech support services. Victims are often tricked into providing personal details, resetting passwords, or granting remote access to their mobile devices. Vishing attacks have become more sophisticated, with attackers using artificial intelligence (AI) and deepfake technology to mimic real voices, making scams harder to detect.

Malicious mobile applications also serve as a major phishing vector. Attackers create fake apps that appear legitimate, often mimicking banking, shopping, or social media applications. Once installed, these apps prompt users to enter their login credentials, which are then sent directly to cybercriminals. Some apps also contain hidden malware that records keystrokes, captures screenshots, or steals authentication tokens. Even apps downloaded from official app stores can sometimes contain security vulnerabilities, making it crucial for users to verify app legitimacy before installation.

To combat mobile phishing and identity theft, users and organizations must adopt strong security practices and awareness strategies. One of the most effective defenses against phishing attacks is multi-factor authentication (MFA), which adds an extra layer of security beyond passwords. Even if attackers manage to steal credentials, they will be unable to access accounts without the second authentication factor, such as a one-time passcode (OTP) sent to a mobile device or biometric verification.

Mobile security solutions, including anti-phishing software and endpoint protection, can help detect and block phishing attempts before they reach users. Some mobile security tools analyze incoming messages and links for suspicious activity, warning users of potential threats. Organizations can also implement email filtering and domain authentication technologies, such as Domain-based Message Authentication, Reporting, and Conformance (DMARC), to reduce phishing emails from reaching employee inboxes.

User education and awareness play a crucial role in preventing mobile phishing attacks. Many phishing attempts succeed because users are unaware of the risks or fail to recognize warning signs. Regular security training can help individuals identify phishing messages, scrutinize URLs before clicking, and verify sender authenticity before responding to requests for sensitive information. Companies should conduct simulated phishing tests to assess employee vulnerability and reinforce good security practices.

To mitigate risks associated with malicious mobile apps, users should only download apps from official app stores, such as Google Play and the Apple App Store, and check app reviews, developer information, and requested permissions before installation. Organizations can implement mobile application management (MAM) and Mobile Device Management (MDM) solutions to prevent employees from installing unauthorized apps on corporate devices.

The role of artificial intelligence (AI) in phishing detection is growing, with AI-driven systems now capable of analyzing vast amounts of data to identify phishing attempts in real time. AI-powered email filters, behavior-based anomaly detection, and natural language processing (NLP) models can help detect fraudulent messages and block them before they reach users. AI can also be used to analyze patterns in phishing campaigns, identifying new attack techniques and enabling security teams to respond proactively.

As mobile phishing techniques become more sophisticated, regulatory frameworks and industry standards are evolving to enhance digital identity protection. Governments and cybersecurity organizations are pushing for stronger identity verification measures, better consumer protection laws, and stricter penalties for cybercriminals engaging in identity theft. Compliance with regulations such as the General Data Protection Regulation (GDPR), the California Consumer Privacy Act (CCPA), and the Payment Services Directive 2 (PSD2) can help protect user data and reduce exposure to phishing threats.

Organizations and individuals must stay vigilant in the face of the growing mobile phishing and identity theft epidemic. By adopting advanced security measures, enhancing awareness, and leveraging cutting-edge technologies, users can protect their mobile identities from cybercriminals seeking to exploit vulnerabilities in digital authentication processes. A proactive approach to mobile security will be crucial in ensuring that digital identities remain secure in an increasingly connected world.

Identity Fraud Prevention

Identity fraud has become one of the most serious cybersecurity threats, affecting individuals, businesses, and financial institutions worldwide. As digital transactions and online interactions increase, cybercriminals continue to develop sophisticated techniques to steal personal information, commit financial fraud, and exploit identity-related vulnerabilities. Preventing identity fraud requires a multi-layered security approach that combines strong authentication measures, real-time fraud detection, regulatory compliance, and user education.

One of the most effective ways to prevent identity fraud is through multi-factor authentication (MFA). Traditional username and password authentication methods are highly vulnerable to phishing attacks, credential stuffing, and brute force attacks. MFA enhances security by requiring users to verify their identity using at least two authentication factors, such as a password (something they know), a smartphone or hardware token (something they have), or biometric authentication (something they are). Even if an attacker obtains login credentials, they would still need an additional authentication factor to access an account, significantly reducing fraud risks.

Biometric authentication is becoming an increasingly popular fraud prevention tool. Fingerprint recognition, facial scanning, and voice authentication provide a higher level of security than passwords or PINs. Since biometric data is unique to each individual and difficult to forge, biometric authentication strengthens identity verification processes for banking, government services, healthcare, and mobile commerce. However, to prevent biometric spoofing and deepfake-based fraud, organizations must implement additional security measures, such as liveness detection and AI-driven anomaly detection.

Behavioral biometrics offers another powerful layer of identity fraud prevention by continuously analyzing user behavior to detect anomalies. Behavioral biometrics monitor factors such as typing speed, touchscreen gestures, mouse movements, and even navigation habits to establish a unique user profile. If a system detects deviations from a user's normal behavior, it can flag the activity as suspicious and trigger additional authentication steps. This continuous authentication approach helps prevent unauthorized access even if an attacker has stolen valid credentials.

Risk-based authentication (RBA) dynamically adjusts authentication requirements based on the risk level associated with a login attempt or transaction. RBA analyzes contextual factors, including device type, geographic location, network security, and past user behavior, to determine whether an authentication request should be treated as high or low risk. If an unusual access attempt is detected, such as a login from a new device or an unexpected location, the system can prompt additional verification steps or temporarily block access until the user's identity is confirmed.

Identity verification technologies are critical for fraud prevention, particularly in industries where identity proofing is required for regulatory compliance. Many financial institutions and online services use document verification techniques, which involve scanning government-issued IDs, passports, or driver's licenses to verify a user's identity. Advanced identity verification platforms incorporate AI-powered optical character recognition (OCR) and facial matching to compare document photos with live selfies, ensuring that the user presenting the ID is its rightful owner.

Fraudsters often exploit synthetic identities, which are created using a combination of real and fake personal information. Synthetic identity fraud is particularly difficult to detect because these identities do not belong to real individuals, making it harder to identify fraudulent activity. Machine learning algorithms and AI-driven fraud detection systems help combat synthetic identity fraud by analyzing behavioral patterns, transaction histories, and identity data inconsistencies. Financial institutions can also cross-reference identity data with trusted sources to detect anomalies and prevent fraudulent account creation.

Tokenization and encryption play a vital role in securing sensitive identity data. Tokenization replaces personal identifiers, such as social security numbers or credit card details, with randomly generated tokens that are meaningless outside the system. Encryption ensures that identity data is protected both in transit and at rest, preventing unauthorized access in case of a data breach. By implementing strong encryption and tokenization techniques, organizations can reduce the exposure of sensitive identity information and prevent data leaks that could lead to fraud.

Identity fraud detection systems leverage artificial intelligence (AI) and big data analytics to identify fraudulent activities in real time. AI-driven fraud detection platforms analyze vast amounts of data to recognize patterns and detect anomalies associated with fraudulent transactions. These systems use machine learning algorithms to continuously refine their detection capabilities, adapting to emerging fraud techniques. Fraud detection tools can monitor financial transactions, login attempts, and online behavior to identify suspicious activities before fraud occurs.

Real-time transaction monitoring is another essential fraud prevention strategy, particularly in financial services and e-commerce. Banks and payment providers use AI-powered fraud detection systems to analyze transaction data in real time and flag potentially fraudulent activities. If an account suddenly exhibits unusual spending patterns, such as large withdrawals, rapid purchases from different locations, or repeated failed login attempts, the system can automatically block the transaction or require additional verification before processing it.

Regulatory compliance and legal frameworks also play a crucial role in identity fraud prevention. Governments and regulatory bodies enforce strict identity verification and fraud prevention regulations, such as Know Your Customer (KYC), Anti-Money Laundering (AML), and the General Data Protection Regulation (GDPR). Businesses must implement identity verification protocols, maintain audit logs, and ensure that customer data is handled securely to comply with these regulations. Failure to meet compliance requirements can result in legal penalties, reputational damage, and financial losses.

Public awareness and user education are critical components of identity fraud prevention. Many fraud cases succeed because individuals unknowingly fall for phishing scams, share personal information with unverified sources, or use weak passwords. Organizations should educate their customers and employees on best practices for protecting personal information, recognizing fraudulent emails or messages, and using security tools such as password managers and two-factor authentication (2FA). Conducting simulated phishing exercises and security training programs can help individuals become more vigilant against identity fraud schemes.

Collaboration between organizations and security professionals is essential to combat identity fraud on a larger scale. Banks, financial institutions, technology providers, and government agencies must work together to share threat intelligence, exchange fraud indicators, and develop security standards that enhance identity protection. Initiatives such as federated identity management and decentralized identity solutions aim to reduce reliance on traditional identity verification methods and provide users with greater control over their personal data.

The rise of decentralized identity (DID) and blockchain-based identity verification offers promising solutions for reducing identity fraud. Decentralized identity systems allow individuals to store and control their identity credentials securely, reducing the risk of centralized data breaches. Verifiable credentials stored on blockchain networks enable secure identity verification without exposing sensitive personal information to third-party providers. By adopting decentralized identity frameworks, businesses can enhance security while giving users more control over their identity data.

Identity fraud prevention requires a proactive and adaptive security strategy that evolves alongside emerging threats. By implementing strong authentication methods, leveraging AI-driven fraud detection, enforcing regulatory compliance, and raising awareness about security best practices, organizations can minimize identity fraud risks and protect both individuals and businesses from financial losses and reputational damage. A combination of advanced security technologies and user education will be essential in the ongoing fight against identity fraud in an increasingly digital world.

Compliance and Regulatory Challenges

As digital identity management evolves, organizations must navigate an increasingly complex landscape of compliance and regulatory challenges. Governments and regulatory bodies worldwide have introduced stringent laws to protect personal data, ensure secure identity verification, and prevent fraud. While these regulations aim to strengthen privacy and security, they also create challenges for businesses that must adapt to evolving compliance requirements while maintaining seamless user experiences.

One of the most significant regulatory frameworks affecting identity management is the General Data Protection Regulation (GDPR), which governs data privacy and security within the European Union (EU). GDPR mandates that organizations handling EU citizens' personal data must implement strict security measures, obtain user consent for data processing, and ensure transparency in data collection and usage. Non-compliance can result in substantial fines, reaching up to 4% of a company's annual revenue. Organizations must adopt privacy-by-design principles, encrypt personal data, and provide users with control over their identity information to comply with GDPR's stringent requirements.

In the United States, identity management is governed by multiple regulations, including the California Consumer Privacy Act (CCPA), which grants consumers the right to know what personal data is being collected, request data deletion, and opt out of data sales. Unlike GDPR, CCPA applies primarily to large businesses operating in California, but its principles have influenced broader privacy regulations across the U.S. The fragmented nature of U.S. data privacy laws presents challenges for organizations, as they must comply with different regulations depending on the states in which they operate.

Know Your Customer (KYC) and Anti-Money Laundering (AML) regulations impose additional compliance challenges, particularly for financial institutions, fintech companies, and cryptocurrency exchanges. KYC regulations require businesses to verify customer identities before providing financial services, reducing the risk of fraud, money laundering, and terrorist financing. Identity verification processes under KYC often involve government-issued ID checks, biometric authentication, and document verification. However, compliance can be resource-intensive, requiring investment in identity verification technologies and customer onboarding solutions.

Another critical regulatory framework is the Payment Services Directive 2 (PSD2), which governs financial transactions within the European Economic Area (EEA). PSD2 introduces Strong Customer Authentication (SCA) requirements, mandating multi-factor authentication (MFA) for online payments and banking transactions. This regulation aims to reduce fraud and enhance security, but it also presents challenges for merchants and payment processors who must implement compliant authentication flows without introducing excessive friction for customers.

In the healthcare sector, the Health Insurance Portability and Accountability Act (HIPAA) in the U.S. sets strict requirements for protecting patient identity and health records. Healthcare providers, insurers, and third-party vendors must ensure secure identity verification, access control, and encryption of electronic health records (EHRs) to comply with HIPAA. Violations can lead to severe financial penalties and reputational damage, making compliance a top priority for organizations handling medical data.

Cross-border identity verification presents another major regulatory challenge. Many businesses operate globally, requiring them to comply with multiple identity regulations across different jurisdictions. Ensuring secure identity verification while adhering to diverse legal frameworks can be complex, particularly when data transfer restrictions apply. For example, GDPR imposes strict rules on transferring personal data outside the EU, requiring organizations to implement mechanisms such as Standard Contractual Clauses (SCCs) or Binding Corporate Rules (BCRs) to ensure data protection.

The rise of biometric authentication and AI-driven identity verification has introduced new compliance concerns regarding ethical use, bias, and data security. Regulations such as the Biometric Information Privacy Act (BIPA) in Illinois, U.S., require companies to obtain explicit user consent before collecting biometric data and impose strict guidelines on data storage and retention. As biometric technologies continue to expand in identity management, organizations must balance security benefits with legal obligations and ethical considerations.

Another compliance challenge involves decentralized identity (DID) and blockchain-based identity verification. While decentralized identity solutions enhance user privacy and security by allowing individuals to control their identity credentials, they also raise questions about legal recognition, regulatory oversight, and liability. Governments and regulatory bodies have yet to establish clear guidelines on how decentralized identity frameworks should be governed, creating uncertainty for businesses looking to adopt these technologies.

Organizations must also address third-party risk management and vendor compliance. Many businesses rely on identity verification providers, cloud services, and authentication platforms to manage digital identities. Ensuring that third-party vendors comply with regulatory requirements is critical to maintaining overall compliance. Companies must conduct vendor risk assessments, review data protection agreements, and implement security audits to verify that third-party identity solutions align with legal and regulatory standards.

The increasing adoption of Zero Trust security models has regulatory implications as well. Zero Trust frameworks enforce continuous authentication, least-privilege access, and real-time monitoring to prevent unauthorized access. While Zero Trust enhances security, organizations must ensure that their implementation aligns with data protection laws, particularly when monitoring user behavior and tracking identity-related activities. Transparency and compliance with employee privacy rights are essential to avoid regulatory violations.

In response to growing compliance challenges, businesses are investing in regulatory technology (RegTech) solutions that automate compliance processes, monitor regulatory changes, and streamline identity verification. AI-driven compliance tools can analyze global regulatory requirements, flag potential risks, and ensure that identity management practices remain up to date with evolving laws. These technologies help organizations reduce compliance costs while maintaining security and regulatory alignment.

Despite the complexities of compliance and regulatory challenges in identity management, organizations can take proactive steps to ensure adherence to legal requirements while protecting user privacy and security. Implementing privacy-by-design principles, enhancing data encryption, maintaining audit logs, and leveraging AI-powered compliance solutions can help businesses navigate the regulatory landscape effectively. By staying informed about global identity regulations and adopting best practices, organizations can build secure, compliant identity management frameworks that align with evolving legal and security standards.

GDPR and Mobile Identity

The General Data Protection Regulation (GDPR) is one of the most comprehensive and stringent data protection laws in the world, designed to safeguard the privacy and personal data of individuals within the European Union (EU). Since its enforcement in May 2018, GDPR has had a profound impact on how organizations collect, process, and store personal data. As mobile devices become central to digital identity management, businesses must ensure that mobile identity solutions comply with GDPR requirements. Mobile identity involves the use of smartphones, biometric authentication, and mobile applications for identity verification, making compliance with data protection laws critical to maintaining user trust and avoiding regulatory penalties.

One of the core principles of GDPR is data minimization, which requires organizations to collect only the personal data necessary for a specific purpose. This principle directly affects mobile identity solutions, as mobile applications and identity verification services must ensure that they do not request excessive or unnecessary personal information from users. For example, a mobile banking app that requires identity verification should only collect essential data such as name, date of birth, and government-issued ID, rather than requesting additional sensitive details unrelated to the service being provided. Organizations implementing mobile identity solutions must evaluate their data collection practices to ensure compliance with GDPR's data minimization requirements.

Another fundamental aspect of GDPR is user consent and transparency. Organizations must obtain explicit, informed, and freely given consent before collecting and processing personal data. In the context of mobile identity, this means that apps and digital services must provide clear explanations of why they need specific identity information, how it will be used, and whether it will be shared with third parties. Consent requests should be written in simple and understandable language, avoiding complex legal jargon that could mislead users. Additionally, mobile identity solutions must offer users the ability to withdraw consent at any time, and organizations must respect such requests without penalizing the user.

Data security and encryption are critical to GDPR compliance, particularly when handling mobile identity data. Mobile devices are inherently vulnerable to security threats such as malware, phishing attacks, and device theft. GDPR mandates that organizations implement strong security measures to protect personal data from unauthorized access, loss, or breaches. This includes encrypting sensitive identity data both in transit and at rest, ensuring that mobile applications use secure authentication protocols, and implementing device security policies such as remote wiping for lost or stolen devices. Businesses that fail to secure mobile identity data adequately may face severe financial penalties under GDPR.

Under GDPR's right to access and data portability, individuals have the right to request access to their personal data and obtain a copy of it in a structured, commonly used, and machine-readable format. Mobile identity solutions must ensure that users can easily retrieve their identity data upon request. For example, if a user registers with a mobile identity provider, they should be able to download a copy of their personal information and transfer it to another service provider without restrictions. Identity providers must also allow users to verify the accuracy of their stored data and request corrections if needed.

Another important GDPR requirement is the right to be forgotten (data erasure), which allows users to request the deletion of their personal data when it is no longer necessary for the original purpose of collection. This poses challenges for mobile identity solutions that store user data for authentication and verification purposes. Organizations must establish clear policies and procedures for handling data deletion requests while ensuring that legal and regulatory obligations are met. For instance, while GDPR allows users to request data deletion, certain laws may require businesses to retain identity records for compliance purposes, such as financial regulations that mandate record-keeping for a specific period. Balancing these requirements is essential for GDPR-compliant mobile identity management.

Third-party data sharing and processing also require strict compliance with GDPR. Many mobile identity solutions rely on third-party verification services, cloud providers, and identity brokers to authenticate users. GDPR mandates that organizations enter into data processing agreements (DPAs) with any third party handling personal data on their behalf. These agreements must define the roles and responsibilities of each party, ensuring that data processors adhere to GDPR's security and privacy requirements. Additionally, organizations must inform users if their personal data will be shared with external entities and provide options to control or limit such sharing.

Cross-border data transfers present another compliance challenge for mobile identity providers. GDPR restricts the transfer of personal data outside the European Economic Area (EEA) unless the receiving country provides an adequate level of data protection. Mobile identity solutions operating across multiple regions must ensure that international data transfers comply with GDPR's safeguards, such as using Standard Contractual Clauses (SCCs) or obtaining user consent before transferring data to non-compliant jurisdictions. Failure to meet these requirements can result in legal consequences and reputational damage.

GDPR compliance also intersects with biometric authentication and mobile identity verification. Many mobile identity solutions use facial recognition, fingerprint scanning, and voice authentication for user verification. However, GDPR classifies biometric data as a special category of personal data, requiring organizations to implement additional security measures and obtain explicit user consent before processing such data. This means that mobile identity providers must ensure that biometric data is stored securely, processed only for legitimate purposes, and deleted when no longer necessary.

To ensure ongoing compliance with GDPR, organizations must conduct regular privacy impact assessments (PIAs) and data protection audits. These assessments help identify potential risks in mobile identity management and evaluate whether data processing activities align with GDPR's principles. By proactively assessing risks and implementing corrective measures, businesses can avoid compliance failures and improve overall data protection practices.

As mobile identity continues to evolve, GDPR will play a crucial role in shaping privacy and security standards. Organizations developing mobile identity solutions must adopt a privacy-by-design approach, ensuring that data protection is embedded into the core of their systems from the outset. By prioritizing transparency, user control, data security, and regulatory compliance, businesses can build trust with users while meeting GDPR's strict requirements.

CCPA and Data Protection Laws

The California Consumer Privacy Act (CCPA) is one of the most significant data protection laws in the United States, designed to give California residents greater control over their personal data. Enacted in 2018 and effective from January 1, 2020, CCPA imposes strict requirements on businesses that collect, process, and share personal data. While it primarily applies to companies operating in California, its impact extends far beyond state borders, influencing national and global data protection policies. Alongside the CCPA, various other data protection laws have emerged worldwide, each with unique requirements that shape how organizations handle personal data.

The CCPA grants consumers several fundamental rights concerning their personal data. One of the most important is the right to know, which allows individuals to request information about the data a business has collected on them, how it is used, and whether it has been shared with third parties. Businesses must provide detailed disclosures upon request, ensuring transparency in data collection and processing. This requirement forces companies to maintain accurate records of data processing activities, creating additional compliance obligations for organizations handling large volumes of consumer data.

Another key provision of the CCPA is the right to delete, which enables consumers to request that businesses erase their personal data. Companies must comply with these requests unless the data is necessary for specific business purposes, such as completing transactions, fulfilling legal obligations, or detecting security threats. While this provision enhances consumer privacy, it also presents challenges for businesses that must develop efficient mechanisms to process deletion requests while ensuring compliance with other regulatory requirements.

The right to opt out of data sales is another significant aspect of the CCPA. Consumers can direct businesses not to sell their personal information to third parties, and companies must provide a clear and accessible way for users to exercise this right. Businesses subject to CCPA must include a "Do Not Sell My Personal Information" link on their websites, allowing users to opt out easily. This regulation has forced companies to reassess their data-sharing practices, particularly those that rely on targeted advertising and third-party data monetization strategies.

CCPA also includes provisions for the protection of minors' data. Businesses must obtain explicit consent from individuals under 16 before selling their personal data, and parental consent is required for users under 13. These rules align with broader child data protection initiatives, such as the Children's Online Privacy Protection Act (COPPA), which governs how businesses collect and use data from children under 13. Organizations handling children's data must implement additional safeguards to ensure compliance with both CCPA and federal regulations.

A critical component of CCPA compliance is data security and breach notification. While the law does not mandate specific security measures, it holds businesses accountable for protecting consumer data. If a company fails to implement reasonable security measures and experiences a data breach, consumers have the right to take legal action. This provision encourages businesses to adopt stronger cybersecurity practices, including encryption, access controls, and threat detection systems, to minimize the risk of data breaches and regulatory penalties.

The enforcement of CCPA falls under the jurisdiction of the California Attorney General, who has the authority to investigate violations and impose fines. Non-compliant businesses may face penalties of up to $7,500 per intentional violation and $2,500 per unintentional violation. While these fines may seem moderate compared to GDPR's more severe penalties, the reputational damage and potential lawsuits resulting from non-compliance can be far more costly for businesses.

CCPA has set a precedent for other U.S. states to introduce similar privacy laws. In 2023, the California Privacy Rights Act (CPRA) expanded CCPA's provisions, strengthening consumer rights and introducing new regulations on sensitive personal data. Other states, including Virginia, Colorado, and Connecticut, have enacted their own privacy laws, creating a fragmented regulatory landscape that businesses must navigate. The lack of a unified federal privacy law in the U.S. means companies must comply with multiple state-level regulations, increasing complexity and compliance costs.

Beyond the U.S., data protection laws such as the General Data Protection Regulation (GDPR) in the European Union have influenced global privacy standards. GDPR, which took effect in 2018, imposes strict data protection requirements, including explicit user consent, the right to data portability, and strict security measures. While GDPR and CCPA share common principles, GDPR applies more broadly to businesses worldwide that process EU citizens' data, whereas CCPA specifically targets companies operating in California.

Other countries have also implemented their own data protection regulations. Brazil's Lei Geral de Proteção de Dados (LGPD), Canada's Personal Information Protection and Electronic Documents Act (PIPEDA), and Japan's Act on the Protection of Personal Information (APPI) all reflect the growing global emphasis on consumer privacy and data security. Businesses operating internationally must ensure compliance with these diverse regulations, requiring robust data governance frameworks and adaptable compliance strategies.

To comply with CCPA and other data protection laws, businesses must adopt privacy-first approaches to data management. Implementing privacy-by-design principles, which integrate data protection into the development of products and services, helps organizations meet regulatory requirements while enhancing consumer trust. Companies should also conduct regular data audits to assess what personal data they collect, how it is stored, and whether it is necessary for business operations. Minimizing data collection and retention reduces regulatory risks and enhances security.

Another essential compliance measure is consumer education and transparency. Businesses must ensure that privacy policies are clear, easily accessible, and written in simple language. Providing users with detailed information about data collection practices, third-party sharing, and security measures helps build trust and ensures compliance with disclosure requirements. Organizations should also invest in consumer-friendly data management tools, allowing users to access, modify, or delete their data easily.

Technology solutions such as data protection automation and compliance management platforms can help businesses navigate the complexities of data privacy regulations. AI-powered tools can monitor compliance risks, flag potential violations, and streamline data access and deletion requests. Implementing encryption, anonymization, and tokenization further strengthens data security, ensuring that personal information is protected from unauthorized access and breaches.

As regulatory landscapes continue to evolve, businesses must remain proactive in their approach to data privacy and compliance. Keeping up with legislative changes, collaborating with legal experts, and adopting flexible data protection frameworks will be crucial for navigating the complexities of CCPA and other global data protection laws. By prioritizing privacy, organizations can not only comply with legal requirements but also enhance customer trust and protect sensitive information in an increasingly data-driven world.

Security Frameworks for Mobile Identity

As mobile devices become central to digital identity management, ensuring secure authentication and data protection is critical. The rise of mobile identity solutions has introduced new challenges, including device security risks, identity fraud, and unauthorized access to sensitive information. To address these concerns, organizations rely on security frameworks designed to establish best practices, enforce access controls, and enhance the integrity of mobile identity systems. These frameworks provide structured guidelines for securing mobile identity authentication, ensuring compliance with regulatory requirements, and mitigating cybersecurity threats.

One of the most widely adopted security frameworks for mobile identity is the Zero Trust Architecture (ZTA). The Zero Trust model operates on the principle that no device or user should be trusted by default, regardless of whether they are inside or outside an organization's network. In mobile identity management, ZTA ensures that every access request is verified continuously through multiple layers of authentication. This approach incorporates risk-based authentication (RBA), multi-factor authentication (MFA), and behavioral analytics to validate user identity dynamically. Zero Trust frameworks also integrate least-privilege access controls, ensuring that mobile users are granted only the minimum permissions necessary to perform their tasks.

Another essential framework is the National Institute of Standards and Technology (NIST) Cybersecurity Framework (CSF), which provides a structured approach to managing cybersecurity risks, including mobile identity security. NIST CSF is built around five core functions: Identify, Protect, Detect, Respond, and Recover. Within mobile identity management, NIST CSF helps organizations define identity verification policies, implement strong encryption methods, and establish continuous monitoring for unauthorized access. The framework also emphasizes biometric authentication, cryptographic security measures, and secure application development to protect mobile identities from cyber threats.

In the financial and payment sectors, the Payment Card Industry Data Security Standard (PCI DSS) establishes security guidelines for mobile payment identity verification. PCI DSS compliance ensures that mobile identity solutions used in payment processing adhere to strict encryption, authentication, and data protection standards. Mobile identity authentication for financial transactions must meet PCI DSS requirements, including strong encryption of stored and transmitted cardholder data, two-factor authentication (2FA) for sensitive operations, and secure application development practices. Organizations using mobile identity for digital payments must follow PCI DSS guidelines to reduce the risk of data breaches and financial fraud.

The Fast Identity Online (FIDO) Alliance standards have played a significant role in shaping security frameworks for mobile identity authentication. FIDO2, an open authentication standard, enables passwordless authentication through biometrics, hardware security keys, and cryptographic authentication methods. FIDO-compliant mobile identity solutions replace traditional password-based authentication with public key cryptography, ensuring that user credentials cannot be intercepted or reused. By eliminating password-based vulnerabilities, FIDO authentication enhances mobile identity security while improving user convenience.

Another crucial security framework is ISO/IEC 27001, an international standard for information security management systems (ISMS). ISO 27001 provides best practices for securing identity and access management (IAM) systems, ensuring that mobile identity solutions comply with global security standards. Organizations adopting ISO 27001 implement data encryption, secure key management, access control policies, and continuous security assessments to protect mobile identity credentials. Compliance with ISO 27001 enhances trust and demonstrates a commitment to robust identity security practices.

The OpenID Connect (OIDC) and OAuth 2.0 protocols are foundational frameworks for secure mobile identity authentication and authorization. OpenID Connect enables single sign-on (SSO) authentication for mobile applications, allowing users to verify their identity across multiple services with a single login. OAuth 2.0, on the other hand, governs secure API access and delegated authentication, ensuring that mobile applications access user data securely without exposing login credentials. By integrating OIDC and OAuth 2.0, mobile identity frameworks ensure secure authentication, reduced credential exposure, and seamless cross-platform identity verification.

Mobile identity security also benefits from the Cloud Security Alliance (CSA) Mobile Security Framework, which provides best practices for securing mobile devices, applications, and identity authentication processes. CSA's framework emphasizes mobile device management (MDM), secure app development, identity governance, and threat monitoring to ensure that mobile identity solutions remain resilient against cyber threats. The framework is particularly relevant for enterprises implementing bring-your-own-device (BYOD) policies, ensuring that personal mobile devices used for authentication comply with security standards.

In the public sector, the Federal Identity, Credential, and Access Management (FICAM) framework provides security guidelines for government agencies managing mobile identity verification. FICAM ensures that digital identity solutions meet federal security and compliance requirements, incorporating multi-factor authentication, biometric identity proofing, and risk-based access controls. The framework also aligns with the National Institute of Standards and Technology (NIST) Special Publication 800-63, which outlines federal digital identity guidelines for mobile authentication and identity proofing.

Decentralized identity frameworks, such as self-sovereign identity (SSI) and blockchain-based identity verification, are gaining traction as secure alternatives to traditional mobile identity management. Decentralized identity solutions allow users to store, manage, and verify their identity credentials on blockchain networks, reducing reliance on centralized identity providers. By leveraging distributed ledger technology (DLT), verifiable credentials, and cryptographic security, decentralized identity frameworks enhance privacy, security, and user control over mobile identity authentication. Organizations exploring decentralized identity solutions must consider regulatory challenges, interoperability with existing IAM frameworks, and scalability concerns.

Security frameworks for mobile identity must also address biometric authentication security, ensuring that fingerprint recognition, facial scanning, and voice authentication meet industry standards for accuracy and fraud prevention. Organizations implementing biometric authentication must comply with biometric data privacy laws, such as the Biometric Information Privacy Act (BIPA) in Illinois, USA, which mandates user consent and secure biometric data storage. Additionally, biometric security frameworks must incorporate liveness detection, spoof detection, and AI-driven fraud analysis to prevent biometric spoofing attacks.

To ensure compliance with security frameworks, organizations should conduct regular security audits, penetration testing, and risk assessments to identify vulnerabilities in mobile identity authentication systems. Continuous security monitoring, real-time threat detection, and adaptive authentication mechanisms enhance mobile identity security by mitigating emerging cyber threats.

As cyber threats targeting mobile identity continue to evolve, security frameworks must adapt to emerging technologies, including artificial intelligence (AI)-driven fraud detection, behavioral biometrics, and privacy-enhancing technologies (PETs). AI-powered identity analytics improve authentication accuracy, detect anomalies, and prevent unauthorized access by analyzing user behavior patterns. Privacy-enhancing technologies, such as homomorphic encryption and zero-knowledge proofs (ZKPs), enable secure identity verification without exposing sensitive personal data.

Organizations adopting mobile identity solutions must integrate security frameworks, regulatory compliance requirements, and emerging authentication technologies to build resilient identity ecosystems. By aligning mobile identity management with industry-recognized security standards, businesses, governments, and financial institutions can enhance trust, reduce fraud risks, and provide secure, user-friendly authentication experiences across mobile platforms.

Mobile Identity in the Cloud Era

The rapid adoption of cloud computing has transformed the way organizations manage digital identities, enabling more scalable, flexible, and secure identity verification processes. In the cloud era, mobile identity plays a crucial role in ensuring seamless authentication and access control across distributed environments. As businesses shift to cloud-based infrastructure, mobile identity solutions must integrate with cloud identity platforms to support secure authentication, enable frictionless access to services, and enhance user experience while maintaining strict security standards.

Cloud-based identity management systems provide organizations with centralized control over user authentication, reducing reliance on traditional on-premise identity management solutions. Cloud identity platforms enable single sign-on (SSO), multi-factor authentication (MFA), identity federation, and adaptive access control, allowing users to authenticate securely from their mobile devices. By leveraging cloud-based identity solutions, businesses can simplify identity management processes, improve scalability, and enhance security while enabling users to access applications and services from any location.

One of the key advantages of integrating mobile identity with cloud-based authentication is scalability. Traditional identity management systems often require significant hardware and administrative resources to support growing user bases. Cloud identity platforms, on the other hand, allow businesses to scale authentication services dynamically, accommodating increasing user demands without compromising security or performance. Whether managing corporate employees, remote workers, or customers accessing digital services, cloud-based mobile identity solutions ensure secure and efficient authentication across distributed networks.

Security remains a top priority for mobile identity in the cloud era. Cloud-based authentication frameworks incorporate zero trust security models, ensuring that no user or device is inherently trusted by default. Zero trust identity frameworks require continuous authentication, dynamic risk assessment, and policy-based access controls to prevent unauthorized access. Mobile identity solutions integrated with zero trust architectures enable context-aware authentication, assessing real-time factors such as device security posture, geographic location, and network trustworthiness before granting access to cloud resources.

Multi-factor authentication (MFA) plays a critical role in securing mobile identity within cloud environments. Cloud-based MFA solutions leverage biometric authentication, push notifications, and one-time passcodes (OTPs) to verify user identity, reducing reliance on passwords that are vulnerable to phishing and credential theft. Mobile devices serve as secure authentication factors, enabling users to approve login attempts with a simple tap or biometric scan. Adaptive authentication techniques further enhance security by adjusting authentication requirements based on contextual risk factors, ensuring that authentication remains strong while minimizing user friction.

Cloud-based identity as a service (IDaaS) platforms have emerged as a key enabler of mobile identity security. IDaaS providers offer managed identity and authentication services that integrate with enterprise applications, enabling seamless mobile identity management without the need for complex infrastructure. Leading IDaaS solutions, such as Microsoft Azure Active Directory (Azure AD), Okta, and Google Identity Platform, provide organizations with secure authentication, access control, and identity federation capabilities. These platforms support OAuth 2.0, OpenID Connect (OIDC), and SAML protocols, ensuring interoperability with mobile applications and cloud-based services.

Another important aspect of mobile identity in the cloud era is federated identity management, which enables users to authenticate once and access multiple cloud services without re-entering credentials. Federation protocols such as OpenID Connect, SAML, and WS-Federation allow organizations to establish trusted identity relationships between cloud providers and service providers. This simplifies authentication workflows, reduces password fatigue, and improves security by minimizing password exposure across multiple platforms. Federated identity solutions also enhance employee productivity by providing seamless access to corporate cloud applications using their mobile identity credentials.

The integration of biometric authentication with cloud identity platforms has further strengthened mobile identity security. Cloud-based biometric authentication services enable businesses to verify user identities through fingerprint scanning, facial recognition, and voice authentication, reducing the risk of credential-based attacks. Leading cloud providers, including Amazon Web Services (AWS), Google Cloud, and Microsoft Azure, offer biometric authentication APIs that allow organizations to integrate advanced identity verification capabilities into mobile applications and cloud services.

Despite its benefits, mobile identity in the cloud era also presents challenges related to data privacy, regulatory compliance, and identity governance. Organizations must ensure that mobile identity data stored in the cloud complies with data protection laws such as the General Data Protection Regulation (GDPR), the California Consumer Privacy Act (CCPA), and industry-specific regulations like HIPAA and PCI DSS. Compliance with these regulations requires organizations to implement strong data encryption, secure access controls, and privacy-preserving identity verification methods.

Cloud-based identity governance and administration (IGA) solutions help organizations manage mobile identity lifecycles, ensuring that users have appropriate access permissions while minimizing security risks. IGA platforms enable automated user provisioning, access reviews, and policy enforcement, reducing the risk of unauthorized access and insider threats. By integrating identity analytics and AI-driven risk assessments, organizations can proactively detect and mitigate identity-related security incidents in cloud environments.

Another challenge in mobile identity management within the cloud is managing identity across hybrid and multi-cloud environments. Many organizations use a combination of on-premise, private cloud, and public cloud services, requiring seamless identity integration across different platforms. Cloud-based identity orchestration solutions enable organizations to unify authentication processes across hybrid environments, ensuring consistent access policies, secure identity federation, and centralized user authentication across multiple cloud providers.

The adoption of decentralized identity (DID) and blockchain-based identity verification is gaining traction as a potential solution to enhance privacy and security in cloud-based mobile identity management. Decentralized identity frameworks allow users to control their digital identities independently, without relying on centralized identity providers. By leveraging blockchain technology, users can store verifiable credentials securely on their mobile devices, enabling trustless authentication and reducing reliance on third-party authentication services.

Organizations must also address identity fraud and account takeover (ATO) risks in cloud-based mobile identity systems. AI-driven fraud detection, continuous authentication, and behavioral biometrics help mitigate identity fraud by detecting suspicious login attempts, device anomalies, and credential theft in real-time. Cloud-based fraud prevention solutions analyze user behavior across multiple sessions, enabling proactive identity protection against phishing, credential stuffing, and brute force attacks.

As cloud computing continues to evolve, the future of mobile identity will be shaped by advancements in AI, machine learning, and identity intelligence. AI-powered identity verification algorithms will enhance fraud detection, improve adaptive authentication, and automate identity lifecycle management. Additionally, zero-knowledge proofs (ZKPs) and homomorphic encryption will enable privacy-preserving authentication methods, allowing users to verify their identities without exposing sensitive personal data.

Organizations must adopt security-first approaches to cloud-based mobile identity management, ensuring that authentication mechanisms remain resilient against cyber threats while maintaining compliance with global data protection regulations. By leveraging cloud-native identity solutions, multi-factor authentication, and AI-driven security frameworks, businesses can enhance mobile identity security while providing seamless and secure access to digital services.

IoT and Mobile Identity Management

The proliferation of the Internet of Things (IoT) has transformed the way devices communicate, interact, and authenticate users. With billions of connected devices across industries such as healthcare, finance, transportation, and smart homes, managing identity and access for these devices has become a critical challenge. Mobile identity management (MIM) plays a crucial role in securing IoT ecosystems by enabling seamless authentication, access control, and identity verification for both users and connected devices. As IoT expands, ensuring robust mobile identity management is essential to prevent unauthorized access, data breaches, and cyber threats.

One of the primary challenges in IoT identity management is the sheer volume and diversity of connected devices. Unlike traditional IT environments, where identity management primarily focuses on human users, IoT ecosystems involve a wide range of devices, including smart sensors, wearables, industrial control systems, and autonomous vehicles. Each device requires a unique identity to securely communicate with other devices and cloud services. Mobile identity solutions help bridge the gap between human users and IoT devices by enabling authentication through smartphones, biometrics, and digital identity wallets.

Mobile identity management in IoT environments relies on device authentication and identity provisioning to ensure that only trusted devices can access networks and services. Traditional authentication methods such as passwords and PINs are not feasible for IoT due to scalability and security limitations. Instead, IoT identity management employs certificate-based authentication, cryptographic key exchange, and tokenized access control to verify device identities. Mobile devices serve as an intermediary for registering and provisioning IoT devices, allowing users to authenticate and manage device permissions through secure mobile applications.

Biometric authentication and mobile identity verification enhance security in IoT ecosystems by ensuring that only authorized users can interact with connected devices. For example, in a smart home environment, biometric authentication on a mobile device can be used to unlock doors, control appliances, and authorize secure transactions. Similarly, healthcare IoT devices, such as remote patient monitoring systems, rely on mobile identity verification to ensure that only verified patients and medical professionals can access sensitive health data. By integrating biometrics with IoT identity management, organizations can enhance user trust while preventing unauthorized access.

One of the major security risks in IoT identity management is device impersonation and identity spoofing. Attackers can manipulate IoT devices by cloning device identities, intercepting authentication credentials, or exploiting weak security configurations. To mitigate these risks, IoT security frameworks implement mutual authentication protocols, blockchain-based identity verification, and AI-driven anomaly detection to identify suspicious activity. By leveraging mobile identity solutions, organizations can enforce strong authentication measures, ensuring that each IoT device operates within its designated security policies.

Zero Trust security models play a vital role in securing IoT identity management. Unlike traditional perimeter-based security models that assume trust within a network, Zero Trust enforces continuous authentication, least-privilege access, and dynamic risk assessments for IoT devices. Mobile identity solutions integrated with Zero Trust architectures enable real-time monitoring of IoT authentication requests, blocking unauthorized devices and flagging high-risk activities. This approach minimizes attack surfaces and reduces the risk of IoT-related security breaches.

IoT identity management also requires secure access control mechanisms to regulate device interactions and data sharing. Role-based access control (RBAC) and attribute-based access control (ABAC) frameworks define specific permissions for IoT devices based on user roles, device capabilities, and security policies. For example, in an industrial IoT (IIoT) environment, different levels of access control can be assigned to factory employees, ensuring that only authorized personnel can modify machine configurations or access sensitive operational data. Mobile identity solutions provide a seamless interface for managing access controls, allowing administrators to enforce security policies remotely.

One of the emerging trends in IoT identity management is decentralized identity (DID) and blockchain-based authentication. Decentralized identity frameworks eliminate the need for centralized identity providers by enabling IoT devices to authenticate themselves using self-sovereign identity (SSI) models. Blockchain technology ensures that device identities are immutable, tamper-proof, and verifiable across distributed networks. Mobile identity solutions integrated with decentralized identity frameworks allow users to control and verify device identities without relying on third-party authentication providers, enhancing privacy and security.

As IoT ecosystems grow, regulatory compliance and data protection laws play an increasing role in shaping identity management strategies. Regulations such as the General Data Protection Regulation (GDPR), the California Consumer Privacy Act (CCPA), and industry-specific compliance frameworks like HIPAA and PCI DSS impose strict data protection requirements for IoT identity management. Organizations must ensure that IoT devices comply with encryption standards, data minimization principles, and user consent mechanisms to avoid legal and regulatory penalties. Mobile identity management solutions provide organizations with the necessary tools to enforce compliance, ensuring that IoT devices adhere to global data protection laws.

Another challenge in IoT identity management is securing IoT communication channels to prevent identity-based attacks such as man-in-the-middle (MitM) attacks, replay attacks, and credential interception. Mobile identity solutions incorporate end-to-end encryption, secure tokenization, and public key infrastructure (PKI) authentication to protect IoT identity transactions. Additionally, behavioral analytics and AI-driven threat detection help identify anomalies in IoT authentication patterns, enabling organizations to detect and mitigate potential security threats in real-time.

IoT identity federation is an essential component of interoperable identity management across different IoT platforms. Identity federation enables seamless authentication between IoT devices, cloud services, and enterprise networks using standardized authentication protocols such as OAuth 2.0, OpenID Connect (OIDC), and Security Assertion Markup Language (SAML). Mobile identity management solutions facilitate federated authentication, ensuring that IoT devices can securely access multiple cloud-based services without requiring redundant identity verification.

Looking ahead, artificial intelligence (AI) and machine learning (ML) will play a significant role in IoT identity management, enhancing automated identity verification, fraud detection, and risk assessment. AI-powered mobile identity solutions will analyze IoT device behavior, detect anomalies, and enforce adaptive authentication mechanisms based on contextual intelligence. By leveraging AI-driven insights, organizations can proactively identify identity-based threats and enhance IoT security in dynamic environments.

As IoT ecosystems continue to expand, the role of mobile identity management will become increasingly critical in ensuring secure authentication, access control, and identity governance for connected devices. Organizations must adopt comprehensive identity security strategies, integrate mobile identity solutions with IoT security frameworks, and implement robust authentication mechanisms to mitigate risks associated with IoT identity management. By embracing Zero Trust security models, decentralized identity solutions, and AI-driven threat detection, businesses can build resilient and secure IoT identity ecosystems that protect both users and connected devices.

AI and Machine Learning in Identity Management

Artificial Intelligence (AI) and Machine Learning (ML) are revolutionizing identity management by enhancing security, improving authentication methods, and enabling real-time threat detection. Traditional identity management systems often rely on static authentication methods such as passwords, PINs, and security questions, which are vulnerable to phishing attacks, credential stuffing, and brute force attacks. AI-driven identity management systems provide dynamic and adaptive security mechanisms that continuously analyze user behavior, detect anomalies, and mitigate potential risks. By integrating AI and ML into identity management, organizations can strengthen authentication processes, prevent fraud, and improve overall cybersecurity resilience.

One of the most significant applications of AI in identity management is behavioral biometrics. Unlike traditional biometric authentication methods, such as fingerprint or facial recognition, behavioral biometrics analyze user behavior patterns, including typing speed, mouse movement, touchscreen gestures, and navigation habits. Machine learning algorithms can create a unique behavioral profile for each user, enabling continuous authentication without requiring explicit login credentials. If an anomaly is detected, such as an unusual typing pattern or device interaction, the system can trigger additional verification steps to confirm the user's identity.

Adaptive authentication is another key area where AI enhances identity management. Traditional authentication systems apply the same security measures to all users, regardless of risk level. AI-driven adaptive authentication systems dynamically assess contextual factors such as device type, geographic location, IP address, and past login behavior to determine the appropriate authentication level. If a login attempt is deemed low-risk, the user may be granted access with minimal friction. However, if the system detects a high-risk login attempt—such as access from an unrecognized location or device—it may require multi-factor authentication (MFA) or biometric verification to ensure security.

Machine learning plays a critical role in fraud detection and identity verification. AI-driven fraud detection systems analyze vast amounts of data to identify patterns associated with fraudulent activities, such as unauthorized account access, identity theft, and synthetic identity fraud. These systems use supervised and unsupervised machine learning models to detect anomalies in real-time, allowing security teams to take immediate action. For example, if an AI system detects an unusual login attempt from a country where the user has never been, it can flag the activity and either block access or require additional authentication.

AI-powered risk-based authentication (RBA) further enhances identity security by continuously evaluating the risk level of authentication attempts. RBA systems use machine learning models to assess factors such as failed login attempts, device reputation, and historical user behavior to determine whether a login attempt is genuine or suspicious. If a high-risk login attempt is detected, the system can enforce stricter authentication requirements, such as biometric verification or security challenge questions. By applying AI-driven risk assessment, organizations can reduce friction for legitimate users while preventing unauthorized access.

Another crucial application of AI in identity management is identity proofing and document verification. AI-driven identity verification solutions use computer vision and machine learning to authenticate government-issued IDs, passports, and driver's licenses. These systems analyze document authenticity, detect forgery attempts, and compare ID photos with live selfies using facial recognition. AI-powered document verification is widely used in banking, fintech, healthcare, and e-commerce industries to streamline Know Your Customer (KYC) and Anti-Money Laundering (AML) compliance processes while reducing the risk of identity fraud.

AI is also transforming self-sovereign identity (SSI) and decentralized identity verification. In traditional identity management systems, users rely on centralized identity providers (such as governments or corporations) to authenticate their credentials. AI-driven SSI solutions leverage blockchain technology and verifiable credentials to allow users to control and manage their digital identities independently. Machine learning algorithms enhance decentralized identity verification by analyzing digital signatures, detecting anomalies in credential issuance, and ensuring the integrity of identity transactions. By reducing reliance on centralized identity authorities, AI-powered SSI frameworks improve privacy, security, and user control over personal data.

AI-driven anomaly detection is essential for preventing account takeovers (ATO), phishing attacks, and credential stuffing attacks. Cybercriminals often use automated bots to exploit stolen credentials and gain unauthorized access to user accounts. AI-powered security systems analyze login attempts in real-time, identifying suspicious patterns such as rapid login attempts, repeated failed password entries, and irregular session behavior. By detecting anomalies early, AI helps prevent unauthorized access and reduces the impact of data breaches.

AI and ML also enhance passwordless authentication solutions. Traditional passwords are a major security vulnerability due to weak password habits, reuse across multiple sites, and phishing risks. AI-powered passwordless authentication methods use biometrics, behavioral analytics, cryptographic keys, and risk-based authentication to verify user identity without requiring passwords. These authentication systems adapt to user behavior over time, ensuring that identity verification remains secure, frictionless, and resistant to cyber threats.

Machine learning algorithms are increasingly used for identity analytics and identity governance. AI-driven identity governance platforms help organizations manage user access, enforce security policies, and detect insider threats. These systems analyze user access patterns, flag unusual permissions, and recommend security improvements to ensure that users only have the access they need. By automating role-based access control (RBAC) and attribute-based access control (ABAC), AI enhances identity governance and reduces the risk of privilege escalation and unauthorized data access.

The integration of AI into continuous authentication further strengthens identity security by monitoring user behavior throughout an active session. Unlike traditional authentication methods that verify identity only at login, continuous authentication systems use AI to assess keystroke dynamics, device posture, geolocation, and network security in real-time. If the system detects suspicious activity or deviation from normal behavior, it can enforce additional authentication steps or terminate the session to prevent identity compromise.

Despite its many benefits, AI-driven identity management also presents challenges. Bias in machine learning models, ethical concerns, and data privacy risks must be addressed to ensure that AI-powered identity systems remain fair, transparent, and compliant with global regulations. AI models trained on biased data can lead to inaccurate identity verification results, disproportionately affecting certain user demographics. Organizations must implement bias detection, algorithmic transparency, and fairness audits to mitigate these risks.

AI-powered identity management systems must also comply with data protection laws such as the General Data Protection Regulation (GDPR), the California Consumer Privacy Act (CCPA), and industry-specific regulations like HIPAA and PCI DSS. Organizations must ensure that AI-driven identity verification processes adhere to data minimization, consent requirements, and encryption standards to protect user privacy.

As AI and machine learning continue to evolve, their role in identity management, authentication, and fraud prevention will become even more critical. AI-driven identity security solutions will incorporate explainable AI (XAI), federated learning, and privacy-enhancing technologies to improve accuracy, scalability, and compliance. By leveraging AI for identity proofing, continuous authentication, and real-time threat detection, organizations can build resilient, intelligent, and adaptive identity security frameworks that protect users from emerging cyber threats.

User Experience and Mobile Identity

Mobile identity has transformed the way users authenticate themselves, access services, and interact with digital platforms. As security requirements become more stringent, balancing user experience (UX) with strong authentication has become a critical challenge. A seamless and intuitive mobile identity experience ensures that users can access their accounts and complete transactions without unnecessary friction while maintaining high security standards. Organizations that prioritize user-friendly authentication methods can enhance customer satisfaction, reduce abandonment rates, and improve overall engagement with their services.

One of the key factors influencing user experience in mobile identity is authentication simplicity. Traditional login methods, such as passwords and security questions, are increasingly being replaced with more intuitive alternatives, including biometric authentication, single sign-on (SSO), and passwordless authentication. Users expect quick and hassle-free authentication, and forcing them to remember complex passwords or go through multiple authentication steps can lead to frustration. Biometric authentication, such as fingerprint scanning, facial recognition, and voice authentication, provides a faster and more secure alternative, allowing users to authenticate themselves in seconds without entering passwords.

Single sign-on (SSO) solutions further enhance the mobile identity experience by enabling users to authenticate once and access multiple applications without needing to log in separately for each service. SSO reduces login fatigue and eliminates the need for users to manage multiple credentials. By integrating federated identity protocols like OpenID Connect (OIDC) and Security Assertion Markup Language (SAML), organizations can provide users with a seamless authentication experience across different platforms while ensuring strong security measures.

Passwordless authentication is gaining popularity as a way to improve both security and user experience. Instead of requiring traditional passwords, passwordless authentication relies on cryptographic keys, biometrics, and mobile push notifications to verify user identity. This approach eliminates the risks associated with password-based authentication, such as phishing attacks and credential reuse, while streamlining the login process. Users no longer need to remember or reset passwords, making authentication faster and more convenient.

Another crucial aspect of user experience in mobile identity is frictionless multi-factor authentication (MFA). While MFA enhances security by requiring multiple authentication factors, it can sometimes introduce unnecessary complexity if not implemented correctly. A well-designed MFA solution should provide adaptive authentication, which dynamically adjusts security requirements based on user behavior, device security posture, and contextual risk factors. For example, a trusted user logging in from their usual device may only need biometric authentication, while a suspicious login attempt from an unrecognized device may require additional verification, such as a one-time passcode (OTP) sent to the user's mobile device.

Consistency across devices and platforms is another important factor in mobile identity UX. Users expect a uniform authentication experience whether they are accessing a service from a smartphone, tablet, or desktop. Inconsistent identity verification methods across different devices can lead to confusion and frustration. Organizations must ensure that mobile identity solutions provide a seamless cross-platform experience, allowing users to transition between devices without repeatedly authenticating themselves. Implementing device synchronization and session continuity enables users to move between mobile apps and web applications without unnecessary interruptions.

User onboarding and identity verification also play a significant role in mobile identity UX. Many services require users to verify their identity before granting access to sensitive information or financial transactions. The onboarding process should be fast, secure, and user-friendly, leveraging AI-powered document verification, biometric authentication, and digital identity wallets to streamline identity proofing. Traditional identity verification methods that require users to upload documents, wait for manual approval, or complete multiple verification steps can create frustration and lead to drop-offs. AI-driven identity verification solutions can reduce friction by instantly validating government-issued IDs, performing facial recognition matching, and automating approval processes.

Security transparency and user trust are essential components of a positive mobile identity experience. Users need to feel confident that their personal data is protected and that authentication processes are secure. Organizations should provide clear explanations about how identity data is collected, stored, and used. Implementing privacy-by-design principles ensures that users have control over their identity information, with options to manage their authentication preferences, review access logs, and revoke permissions when necessary. By prioritizing transparency and data protection, businesses can build user trust and encourage higher adoption rates of mobile identity solutions.

Another key factor in improving mobile identity UX is reducing authentication fatigue. Repeatedly asking users to verify their identity through multiple security steps can lead to frustration and abandonment. Implementing continuous authentication solutions, which verify user identity in the background without requiring constant user intervention, can enhance security while maintaining a seamless experience. Behavioral biometrics, AI-driven anomaly detection, and passive authentication techniques allow systems to verify user identity based on real-time behavior, reducing the need for repeated authentication prompts.

Personalization and user preferences can also enhance the mobile identity experience. Allowing users to choose their preferred authentication method—whether biometric login, push notifications, or hardware security keys—gives them greater control over how they access their accounts. Customizable security settings enable users to adjust authentication strength based on their needs, ensuring a balance between convenience and protection. Providing users with the ability to manage trusted devices, login alerts, and authentication preferences improves overall satisfaction and security awareness.

Accessibility and inclusivity are essential considerations in mobile identity UX. Not all users have the same technical expertise, physical abilities, or access to the latest mobile devices. Mobile identity solutions must be designed to accommodate diverse user needs, including support for screen readers, voice-based authentication for visually impaired users, and alternative authentication methods for individuals with limited mobility. Ensuring that mobile identity systems are compliant with accessibility standards such as the Web Content Accessibility Guidelines (WCAG) ensures that all users can securely authenticate themselves without barriers.

The future of user experience in mobile identity will be driven by advancements in AI, machine learning, and decentralized identity solutions. AI-powered predictive authentication models will improve adaptive authentication by learning user behavior patterns and dynamically adjusting security measures. Decentralized identity (DID) frameworks will give users greater control over their identity data, enabling them to authenticate across services without relying on centralized identity providers. Voice and gesture-based authentication methods will further enhance user convenience, making authentication more intuitive and natural.

Organizations must continue to innovate and optimize mobile identity solutions to strike the right balance between security and usability. By focusing on frictionless authentication, adaptive security, transparency, and user-centric design, businesses can create seamless and secure mobile identity experiences that enhance user engagement, build trust, and protect digital assets.

Identity Privacy and Data Protection

In an increasingly digital world, identity privacy and data protection have become critical concerns for individuals, businesses, and governments. With the growing reliance on mobile identity solutions, cloud-based authentication, and biometric verification, protecting user identity and personal data is more important than ever. Cybercriminals continue to exploit vulnerabilities in identity management systems, leading to data breaches, identity theft, and privacy violations. To address these challenges, organizations must implement robust security measures, adhere to data protection regulations, and adopt privacy-enhancing technologies to safeguard user identities.

The importance of identity privacy is driven by the widespread collection and processing of personal information. Digital identity solutions require users to share sensitive data, including biometric information, government-issued IDs, and behavioral patterns. If this data is not properly secured, it can be exposed to unauthorized access, surveillance, or misuse. Ensuring that users retain control over their identity information is essential to building trust in digital identity systems. Privacy-by-design principles help organizations develop identity solutions that prioritize user consent, minimize data collection, and implement strong encryption mechanisms to protect personal data.

Regulatory compliance plays a key role in identity privacy and data protection. Laws such as the General Data Protection Regulation (GDPR) in the European Union and the California Consumer Privacy Act (CCPA) in the United States impose strict requirements on organizations handling personal data. These regulations mandate that businesses obtain user consent before collecting identity information, provide transparency in data processing, and allow users to request access to or deletion of their personal data. Failure to comply with these regulations can result in significant fines, legal penalties, and reputational damage.

One of the biggest challenges in identity privacy is securing biometric data. Biometric authentication methods, such as facial recognition and fingerprint scanning, offer convenience and enhanced security, but they also introduce new privacy risks. Unlike passwords, which can be changed if compromised, biometric data is permanent and cannot be replaced. If biometric information is leaked in a data breach, it can be exploited for fraud, surveillance, and identity theft. Organizations using biometric authentication must implement secure storage solutions, encryption protocols, and liveness detection mechanisms to prevent biometric spoofing and unauthorized access.

Data minimization and anonymization are essential strategies for reducing privacy risks in identity management. Organizations should collect only the minimum amount of personal data necessary for authentication and service delivery. Anonymization techniques, such as tokenization and pseudonymization, allow businesses to process identity data without exposing real user information. For example, instead of storing a user's full biometric profile, organizations can generate encrypted templates that can be used for authentication without revealing actual biometric data. These approaches help protect user privacy while maintaining security.

Another major concern in identity privacy is the risk of third-party data sharing and surveillance. Many identity verification services rely on third-party providers for authentication, document verification, and fraud prevention. While these services enhance security, they also raise questions about how personal data is shared, stored, and used by external entities. Organizations must conduct third-party risk assessments and implement data processing agreements (DPAs) to ensure that identity data is handled securely and in compliance with privacy regulations. Transparency in data-sharing practices is essential for maintaining user trust.

Decentralized identity (DID) solutions offer a promising alternative to traditional identity management systems by giving users greater control over their personal information. DID frameworks use blockchain technology and cryptographic credentials to allow individuals to manage and verify their identities without relying on centralized identity providers. Instead of storing identity data in large corporate databases, decentralized identity models enable users to keep their credentials in digital wallets on their personal devices. This approach reduces the risk of data breaches, identity theft, and unauthorized tracking. Self-sovereign identity (SSI) principles further enhance privacy by ensuring that users can selectively disclose only the necessary information without exposing their full identity.

Cloud-based identity solutions introduce additional data protection challenges, as identity data is often stored and processed in remote data centers. Organizations using cloud-based authentication must implement end-to-end encryption, strict access controls, and real-time threat detection to prevent unauthorized access. Cloud security frameworks such as Zero Trust Architecture (ZTA) ensure that identity verification processes continuously assess risk, enforce multi-factor authentication (MFA), and monitor user behavior for anomalies. Organizations must also comply with cross-border data transfer regulations to ensure that identity data remains protected when stored in global cloud environments.

Artificial intelligence (AI) and machine learning (ML) are playing an increasing role in identity protection and fraud detection. AI-driven identity verification systems analyze user behavior, detect suspicious login attempts, and prevent fraudulent activities in real-time. While AI enhances security, it also raises ethical concerns about data privacy, algorithmic bias, and surveillance risks. Organizations deploying AI-powered identity solutions must ensure transparency, fairness, and compliance with privacy laws to prevent discrimination and misuse of personal data.

Identity theft and data breaches remain some of the biggest threats to personal privacy. Cybercriminals use phishing attacks, credential stuffing, and social engineering to steal personal information and compromise digital identities. Strong authentication measures, such as passwordless authentication, behavioral biometrics, and hardware security keys, help mitigate the risks of identity theft. Additionally, organizations should implement real-time monitoring, dark web scanning, and identity theft protection services to detect and respond to identity-related threats.

User education and awareness are essential for enhancing identity privacy and data security. Many privacy risks arise from human error, weak passwords, and lack of awareness about data protection best practices. Organizations should educate users on how to recognize phishing attempts, enable two-factor authentication (2FA), and manage privacy settings on mobile devices and online platforms. Providing clear privacy policies, user-friendly security controls, and privacy dashboards empowers individuals to take control of their digital identities.

Looking ahead, privacy-enhancing technologies (PETs) will play a crucial role in identity protection. Innovations such as homomorphic encryption, zero-knowledge proofs (ZKPs), and secure multi-party computation (SMPC) enable authentication and identity verification without exposing personal data. These technologies allow users to prove their identity without revealing sensitive information, ensuring privacy while maintaining security.

Organizations must adopt a privacy-first approach to identity management, integrating data protection principles, encryption technologies, and user control mechanisms into their authentication systems. By prioritizing privacy and compliance, businesses can build secure, transparent, and user-friendly identity solutions that protect individuals from identity fraud, unauthorized data access, and emerging cybersecurity threats.

Future of Mobile Identity

The future of mobile identity is evolving rapidly as advancements in technology, security frameworks, and digital identity management redefine how users authenticate themselves across online platforms. With the increasing reliance on mobile devices for identity verification, authentication, and access control, the next generation of mobile identity solutions will focus on enhancing security, improving user convenience, and ensuring privacy. Innovations such as decentralized identity, artificial intelligence (AI)-driven authentication, biometric security, and blockchain-based verification are set to transform the landscape of mobile identity management in the coming years.

One of the key trends shaping the future of mobile identity is decentralized identity (DID). Traditional identity management systems rely on centralized authorities, such as governments, corporations, or identity providers, to issue and verify identities. However, centralized identity models pose security risks, including data breaches, identity theft, and unauthorized surveillance. Decentralized identity frameworks give users control over their identity credentials, allowing them to manage their digital identity through self-sovereign identity (SSI) models. These solutions use blockchain technology, cryptographic verification, and verifiable credentials to enable secure identity authentication without relying on centralized databases. In the future, DID is expected to reduce identity fraud, enhance privacy, and provide greater user autonomy in digital interactions.

Artificial intelligence (AI) and machine learning (ML) are playing an increasingly significant role in mobile identity verification and fraud detection. AI-driven identity systems analyze vast amounts of data, detect anomalies, and predict potential security threats in real-time. For example, AI-powered authentication solutions can evaluate behavioral biometrics, device intelligence, and contextual factors to continuously verify user identity without requiring manual authentication inputs. Adaptive authentication systems, which dynamically adjust security requirements based on real-time risk assessments, will become more common. These AI-driven solutions will reduce the need for static passwords while enhancing mobile identity security through continuous authentication and predictive risk analysis.

The rise of passwordless authentication is another major shift in the future of mobile identity. Traditional password-based authentication has long been a weak link in security due to password reuse, phishing attacks, and credential stuffing. In the future, passwordless authentication methods, such as biometrics, cryptographic keys, and mobile push notifications, will replace traditional login credentials. Technologies such as FIDO2 authentication, passkeys, and secure enclaves on mobile devices will allow users to authenticate without relying on passwords, reducing the risk of cyber threats while simplifying the user experience.

Biometric authentication is expected to evolve further, expanding beyond fingerprints and facial recognition to include voice authentication, iris scanning, palm recognition, and gait analysis. Advances in multi-modal biometrics will enhance security by combining multiple biometric factors to improve accuracy and prevent spoofing attacks. For example, future smartphones may integrate voice recognition and facial biometrics for multi-factor authentication (MFA) without requiring additional authentication steps. AI-powered biometric authentication will also incorporate liveness detection and anti-spoofing mechanisms, ensuring that biometric data cannot be manipulated by deepfake technology or synthetic identity fraud.

Mobile identity wallets are set to become a mainstream method for storing and managing digital identities. These wallets, which act as secure containers for storing digital IDs, verifiable credentials, and authentication tokens, will allow users to present proof of identity, age, or credentials without exposing unnecessary personal information. Governments and private organizations are already exploring mobile identity wallets for digital driver's licenses, national ID programs, and financial identity verification. Future implementations will leverage blockchain-based identity frameworks and zero-knowledge proofs (ZKPs) to enable privacy-preserving authentication, allowing users to verify attributes (e.g., "I am over 18") without revealing exact details (e.g., birthdate).

The integration of 5G and edge computing will also impact mobile identity, enabling faster and more secure authentication processes. With the expansion of 5G networks, mobile identity solutions will benefit from low-latency authentication, real-time threat detection, and seamless cross-device identity verification. Edge computing will allow mobile identity systems to process authentication requests locally on the device rather than relying on centralized cloud servers, reducing exposure to cyberattacks and enhancing privacy-preserving authentication.

Another major development in mobile identity is the rise of federated identity and identity orchestration. In a world where users interact with multiple online services, federated identity allows seamless authentication across platforms using a single verified identity. Future identity federation models will be powered by AI-driven risk scoring, decentralized identifiers, and self-sovereign credentials, eliminating the need for users to create multiple accounts for different services. Identity orchestration platforms will enable secure cross-platform authentication, ensuring that mobile users can move between applications and devices without friction while maintaining strong security controls.

The concept of Zero Trust security will continue to influence mobile identity frameworks. Zero Trust principles dictate that no user or device should be inherently trusted, requiring continuous authentication, strict access controls, and dynamic risk assessments. In the future, mobile identity systems will integrate context-aware authentication, real-time behavior analysis, and AI-driven risk engines to verify users continuously. Continuous authentication mechanisms will replace static logins, ensuring that access is only granted if user behavior remains consistent and within expected risk thresholds.

Regulatory and compliance challenges will also shape the future of mobile identity. With growing concerns about data privacy, biometric security, and surveillance risks, governments worldwide are implementing stricter identity protection laws and digital identity governance frameworks. GDPR, CCPA, and emerging global regulations will require organizations to implement privacy-by-design principles, user consent mechanisms, and data minimization strategies when managing mobile identities. In response, organizations will adopt privacy-enhancing technologies (PETs), such as homomorphic encryption, differential privacy, and federated learning, to ensure compliance with evolving regulatory requirements.

The future of mobile identity will also see greater adoption of identity verification for the Internet of Things (IoT). As smart devices, connected cars, and industrial IoT (IIoT) systems become more prevalent, mobile identity frameworks will need to extend authentication beyond human users to machines, sensors, and autonomous systems. Secure device identity management, cryptographic authentication, and blockchain-based IoT identity verification will be essential to prevent unauthorized access and IoT-related cyber threats.

As mobile identity continues to evolve, organizations must prepare for the next generation of authentication and identity verification technologies. The shift towards decentralized identity, AI-driven security, passwordless authentication, and biometric innovations will redefine how users interact with digital platforms. Businesses, governments, and technology providers must collaborate to build interoperable, secure, and privacy-preserving identity ecosystems that enhance security while providing seamless user experiences. By embracing emerging technologies and regulatory best practices, the future of mobile identity will be more secure, efficient, and user-centric than ever before.

Case Studies in Mobile Identity Management

The rapid evolution of mobile identity management has led organizations across various industries to implement advanced authentication and access control solutions. Businesses, governments, and financial institutions have increasingly relied on mobile identity to enhance security, streamline user experience, and comply with regulatory requirements. Examining real-world case studies provides insights into how different sectors have successfully deployed mobile identity management solutions to address security challenges and improve digital interactions.

One of the most prominent case studies in mobile identity management comes from Estonia's e-Residency program, which has become a global model for digital identity innovation. Estonia, a leader in digital governance, launched the e-Residency program to enable global entrepreneurs to establish and manage businesses remotely within the country. The program provides users with a mobile-enabled digital identity, allowing them to sign documents, access banking services, and authenticate securely without being physically present in Estonia. This initiative has demonstrated how mobile identity solutions combined with cryptographic authentication and blockchain technology can enable secure, remote digital interactions while maintaining compliance with international regulatory standards.

Another significant case study is India's Aadhaar system, the world's largest biometric identity program. Aadhaar assigns each citizen a 12-digit unique identification number linked to their biometric and demographic data, including fingerprint and iris scans. This identity system has transformed access to government services, banking, and mobile telecommunications in India. Mobile identity authentication is a key component of Aadhaar, allowing users to verify their identity via mobile devices using biometric authentication and one-time passcodes (OTPs). Aadhaar's integration with digital wallets and banking applications has significantly improved financial inclusion, enabling millions of unbanked individuals to access secure financial services. However, concerns over data privacy, security vulnerabilities, and centralized identity control have led to debates about the risks and governance of large-scale biometric identity systems.

In the financial sector, banks and fintech companies have adopted mobile identity solutions to prevent fraud and streamline customer onboarding. One notable example is Revolut, a digital banking platform that uses AI-powered identity verification and biometric authentication to enhance security while simplifying account registration. Revolut leverages facial recognition, document verification, and behavioral biometrics to ensure secure mobile banking access. By automating identity verification with AI, Revolut has reduced onboarding time, minimized fraud risks, and improved customer experience. The case of Revolut highlights how mobile identity verification combined with AI-driven fraud detection can enhance security without introducing excessive friction for users.

The United Kingdom's GOV.UK Verify program serves as another case study in mobile identity for government services. GOV.UK Verify allows citizens to securely access online government services using identity verification providers such as Experian, Barclays, and Post Office. Users authenticate via their mobile devices using multi-factor authentication (MFA), facial recognition, and secure SMS-based verification codes. While GOV.UK Verify has improved digital identity access for citizens, it has also faced challenges related to user adoption, interoperability with private sector identity systems, and authentication reliability. The program's evolution reflects the complexities of implementing nationwide digital identity systems that balance security, usability, and regulatory compliance.

In the healthcare sector, mobile identity management has improved patient data security and access to telemedicine services. One example is France's Carte Vitale system, which provides secure mobile authentication for healthcare services. Patients can use their mobile identity to access electronic health records (EHRs), schedule medical appointments, and verify prescriptions. By integrating mobile-based authentication and biometric verification, France's healthcare system has enhanced data security, reduced medical fraud, and improved convenience for patients and healthcare providers. This case study demonstrates how mobile identity solutions can improve digital healthcare services while ensuring compliance with data protection laws such as GDPR.

Retail and e-commerce have also benefited from mobile identity management, with companies implementing passwordless authentication and biometric payment systems. Amazon One, for example, has introduced palm recognition technology that allows users to make contactless payments using their unique palm print. This mobile identity solution eliminates the need for passwords, PINs, or physical cards, providing a seamless and secure authentication method for consumers. The adoption of biometric payment systems in retail environments highlights the potential of mobile identity to improve customer experience while maintaining strong security measures.

In the transportation and travel industry, mobile identity is streamlining border control and passenger verification. One notable example is the Mobile Passport Control (MPC) program in the United States, which enables U.S. citizens and Canadian visitors to submit passport and customs information via a mobile app before arriving at customs checkpoints. This mobile identity solution reduces wait times, improves efficiency, and enhances security at border crossings. Similarly, airports and airlines are adopting biometric identity verification systems, such as facial recognition boarding at select U.S. airports, allowing travelers to board flights without presenting a physical boarding pass or passport. These case studies illustrate how mobile identity solutions can enhance security and efficiency in global travel and border management.

Cybersecurity firms have also implemented mobile identity authentication to combat phishing attacks and credential theft. Google's Advanced Protection Program (APP) provides an example of how mobile identity and hardware security keys can protect high-risk users, such as journalists, politicians, and business leaders. The program requires users to authenticate via physical security keys or mobile-based authentication tokens, eliminating the risks associated with traditional password-based authentication. Google's approach demonstrates how mobile identity solutions combined with strong authentication mechanisms can mitigate identity-related cyber threats and protect users from account takeovers.

In the corporate sector, mobile identity management has become essential for remote workforce security. With the rise of remote work and cloud-based enterprise applications, companies have adopted Zero Trust security models that enforce continuous authentication, least-privilege access control, and device-based identity verification. Microsoft's Azure Active Directory (Azure AD) provides a case study of how enterprise identity solutions integrate mobile authentication, single sign-on (SSO), and adaptive security policies to protect corporate data. By leveraging mobile identity for conditional access, AI-driven anomaly detection, and device-based security policies, enterprises have enhanced their security posture while enabling employees to work securely from any location.

These case studies illustrate the diverse applications of mobile identity management across different industries, highlighting the benefits and challenges of implementing secure digital identity solutions. Whether improving financial security, enhancing government services, securing enterprise authentication, or streamlining travel processes, mobile identity continues to play a pivotal role in the future of digital authentication and access control. Organizations must continue to adapt and refine their mobile identity strategies to address evolving security threats, regulatory requirements, and user expectations.

Identity Crisis Management

Identity crisis management is a critical component of modern cybersecurity, focusing on detecting, mitigating, and recovering from identity-related security incidents. As digital identity becomes the foundation for accessing services, conducting transactions, and verifying users, the risks associated with identity breaches, fraud, and account takeovers have increased significantly. Organizations must have well-defined strategies to respond to identity crises, minimize damage, and restore trust in their identity management systems. Effective identity crisis management involves proactive monitoring, rapid response protocols, user protection measures, and regulatory compliance to ensure that affected individuals and organizations can recover swiftly from identity threats.

One of the most common identity crises organizations face is account takeover (ATO) attacks, where cybercriminals gain unauthorized access to user accounts by exploiting stolen credentials, phishing attacks, or brute force methods. ATO incidents can lead to financial fraud, data breaches, and reputational damage. Organizations must implement multi-factor authentication (MFA), biometric authentication, and behavioral analytics to prevent unauthorized access. In the event of an ATO, a rapid incident response is necessary, including forcing password resets, revoking compromised session tokens, and alerting affected users about suspicious activity.

Identity theft and data breaches are another major source of identity crises. When personally identifiable information (PII) such as social security numbers, passport details, and credit card information is leaked, cybercriminals can use this data to impersonate individuals, commit financial fraud, or create synthetic identities. Organizations must have a structured breach response plan that includes notifying affected users, collaborating with regulatory authorities, and enhancing security measures to prevent further exploitation. Many jurisdictions, including the General Data Protection Regulation (GDPR) and the California Consumer Privacy Act (CCPA), require organizations to report identity breaches within specific timeframes and provide remedies to impacted individuals.

Phishing attacks remain one of the primary causes of identity-related security incidents. Cybercriminals use phishing emails, SMS messages (smishing), and voice calls (vishing) to trick users into revealing their login credentials or sensitive information. Identity crisis management strategies must include phishing awareness training, email filtering technologies, and AI-driven anomaly detection to prevent phishing-related breaches. In cases where users fall victim to phishing scams, organizations should deploy real-time fraud detection systems, suspend compromised accounts, and guide users through identity recovery steps.

Biometric identity fraud and deepfake attacks pose emerging threats in identity management. As organizations increasingly rely on facial recognition, fingerprint scanning, and voice authentication for secure access, attackers are developing sophisticated techniques to bypass biometric security. Deepfake technology can be used to create realistic voice or video recordings that mimic real individuals, potentially deceiving identity verification systems. Organizations must integrate liveness detection, anti-spoofing algorithms, and AI-powered biometric fraud detection to prevent biometric identity crises. If biometric data is compromised, organizations must provide users with alternative authentication options, such as hardware security keys or behavioral biometrics.

Insider threats and identity misuse can also lead to identity crises within organizations. Employees, contractors, or business partners with privileged access may misuse their credentials to steal data, manipulate systems, or leak sensitive information. Role-based access control (RBAC), attribute-based access control (ABAC), and continuous access monitoring help mitigate insider threats. In cases where an insider threat is detected, organizations must respond immediately by revoking access, conducting forensic investigations, and implementing stricter security policies to prevent future incidents.

A crucial component of identity crisis management is identity recovery and user support. When individuals experience an identity breach or fraudulent activity, they need a clear path to recover their accounts and protect their personal information. Organizations should offer dedicated identity recovery services, fraud resolution support, and secure identity re-verification processes. Implementing automated identity recovery workflows, knowledge-based authentication (KBA) alternatives, and real-time alerts can help users regain access to their accounts quickly and securely.

Regulatory compliance and legal considerations play a significant role in identity crisis management. Organizations must adhere to global and regional identity protection laws, ensuring that they handle identity breaches responsibly. Regulations such as GDPR, CCPA, and Payment Card Industry Data Security Standard (PCI DSS) require businesses to maintain detailed audit logs, implement security best practices, and notify authorities and users of data breaches within specific timelines. Failing to comply with these regulations can result in legal penalties, lawsuits, and reputational harm.

Incident response frameworks and cybersecurity teams are essential in managing identity crises effectively. Organizations should establish Security Operations Centers (SOCs) and Computer Security Incident Response Teams (CSIRTs) to detect, investigate, and mitigate identity-related threats. These teams should develop identity crisis playbooks, outlining step-by-step procedures for handling different types of identity attacks, including credential leaks, social engineering scams, identity fraud, and insider threats. Regular tabletop exercises, penetration testing, and red team simulations help organizations prepare for identity crises and improve their response capabilities.

The rise of decentralized identity solutions offers a potential long-term solution to identity crises. Self-sovereign identity (SSI) frameworks, blockchain-based identity verification, and verifiable credentials enable users to control their digital identities without relying on centralized authorities. Unlike traditional identity systems, where identity providers store vast amounts of personal data, decentralized identity models reduce the risk of large-scale breaches and unauthorized data access. In the future, widespread adoption of decentralized identity solutions could minimize identity-related crises by giving users greater control over their authentication and verification processes.

Artificial intelligence (AI) and machine learning (ML) play an increasingly important role in identity threat detection and crisis management. AI-driven fraud detection systems analyze login patterns, transaction behaviors, and device fingerprints to identify anomalies in real time. Automated identity threat intelligence platforms can detect credential leaks on the dark web, flag suspicious login attempts, and block unauthorized access attempts before they lead to a crisis. AI-powered chatbots and virtual assistants can also assist users in identity recovery, guiding them through account restoration processes and fraud reporting mechanisms.

Public awareness and education are fundamental in reducing identity-related crises. Many identity breaches occur due to human error, lack of cybersecurity awareness, or poor password hygiene. Organizations should invest in security awareness training programs, phishing simulations, and digital identity workshops to educate users on safe identity management practices. Encouraging the use of password managers, multi-factor authentication (MFA), and privacy-preserving authentication methods can significantly reduce the likelihood of identity crises.

The effectiveness of identity crisis management depends on proactive security measures, rapid incident response, and user empowerment. Organizations must continuously adapt to emerging threats, invest in advanced security technologies, and foster a security-first culture to mitigate identity risks and protect users from evolving digital threats.

Identity Federation in 5G Networks

The introduction of 5G networks has revolutionized mobile connectivity, enabling faster speeds, lower latency, and seamless integration of various technologies such as IoT (Internet of Things), cloud computing, and edge computing. As 5G networks expand, secure and scalable identity management has become a critical component of their infrastructure. One of the most promising approaches to managing digital identities in this new era is identity federation, which allows users to access multiple services across different providers using a single authenticated identity. Identity federation in 5G networks enhances security, improves user experience, and ensures compliance with regulatory requirements while maintaining interoperability between different network operators and service providers.

The Role of Identity Federation in 5G Networks

5G networks introduce a more complex ecosystem where users, devices, applications, and services require seamless authentication and access control across multiple domains. Unlike previous generations of mobile networks, 5G is designed to support a vast array of interconnected devices, ranging from smartphones and tablets to IoT devices, smart cities, and autonomous vehicles. Managing identity securely across these diverse endpoints requires federated identity management, where a single authentication mechanism allows users and devices to interact across multiple networks without requiring multiple logins or identity verifications.

Identity federation in 5G networks is facilitated through federated authentication frameworks, which enable different entities, such as telecom operators, cloud providers, and enterprise networks, to trust a shared identity verification process. This is particularly important in network slicing, a key feature of 5G that allows operators to create virtualized network segments with specific security and authentication requirements. Each slice may serve a different industry, such as healthcare, finance, or smart manufacturing, requiring distinct access control mechanisms. Identity federation ensures that users and devices can move securely between these network slices without repeatedly authenticating themselves.

Federated Identity Standards and Protocols in 5G

To achieve interoperability and secure identity federation, 5G networks rely on standardized authentication protocols, including:

OpenID Connect (OIDC): A widely adopted authentication protocol that enables single sign-on (SSO) using OAuth 2.0, allowing users to authenticate across multiple service providers with a single identity.

Security Assertion Markup Language (SAML): Commonly used in enterprise environments, SAML allows secure identity exchange between organizations and can be applied to federated authentication in telecom networks.

OAuth 2.0: A widely used authorization framework that allows users to grant access to their data without exposing login credentials, making it essential for secure device-to-device authentication in 5G environments.

5G Authentication and Key Agreement (5G-AKA): A protocol designed specifically for 5G networks, ensuring strong cryptographic authentication between user devices and network operators while supporting identity federation across different providers.

These protocols enable secure identity federation between mobile carriers, cloud platforms, and enterprise networks, allowing seamless user authentication across multiple domains while maintaining high security standards.

Security and Privacy Challenges in Federated Identity for 5G

While identity federation offers numerous advantages in 5G networks, it also introduces security and privacy challenges that must be addressed. Some of the most pressing concerns include:

Identity Spoofing and Unauthorized Access: Attackers may attempt to forge or manipulate federated credentials to gain unauthorized access to 5G services. Implementing strong cryptographic identity verification and multi-factor authentication (MFA) helps mitigate this risk.

Data Privacy and Regulatory Compliance: 5G identity federation involves cross-border data exchange, raising concerns about compliance with regulations such as GDPR (General Data Protection Regulation), CCPA (California Consumer Privacy Act), and industry-specific privacy laws. Organizations must ensure that federated identity frameworks incorporate data minimization, encryption, and user consent mechanisms.

Decentralized Identity Risks: While federated identity management is often based on centralized identity providers, some 5G implementations explore decentralized identity (DID) and blockchain-based authentication. While this enhances privacy and user control, it also presents challenges related to trust management, interoperability, and governance.

Network Slicing Security: Each 5G network slice may have different security and authentication requirements. Identity federation solutions must ensure that authentication policies remain consistent across slices while adapting to varying levels of security sensitivity.

To address these challenges, telecom operators and identity providers must implement zero-trust security models, ensuring continuous authentication and real-time anomaly detection. AI-powered identity analytics can further enhance security by detecting unusual login behaviors, identity fraud, and session hijacking attempts.

Use Cases for Federated Identity in 5G Networks

Several industries and sectors benefit from identity federation in 5G networks, including:

Smart Cities: In a 5G-powered smart city, federated identity allows residents and visitors to authenticate seamlessly across public Wi-Fi networks, transportation services, and government portals without needing multiple logins.

Enterprise Mobility: Businesses leveraging 5G for remote work and IoT security can integrate federated identity management to enable secure access to cloud applications, VPNs, and enterprise systems from any location.

Healthcare: Federated identity in 5G networks ensures that medical professionals, patients, and connected medical devices can securely exchange health data while complying with privacy regulations such as HIPAA.

Finance and Banking: 5G-enabled financial services benefit from identity federation by enabling secure mobile banking, cross-border transactions, and fraud detection across multiple institutions.

Autonomous Vehicles: Federated identity enables secure vehicle-to-vehicle (V2V) and vehicle-to-infrastructure (V2I) authentication, ensuring that self-driving cars can interact safely with 5G-connected road systems.

The Future of Identity Federation in 5G Networks

As 5G networks continue to expand, the evolution of federated identity solutions will focus on:

AI-Driven Authentication: AI-powered behavioral biometrics and risk-based authentication will enhance federated identity security by adapting authentication requirements in real time based on user behavior.

Decentralized and Self-Sovereign Identity (SSI): Future 5G identity management solutions will explore blockchain-based identity verification and self-sovereign credentials, reducing reliance on centralized identity providers.

Edge Computing Integration: Identity federation will extend to 5G edge computing environments, enabling fast and secure authentication for IoT devices, industrial automation, and low-latency applications.

Cross-Network Identity Interoperability: As global 5G adoption grows, federated identity frameworks will need to support seamless authentication across different telecom providers, cloud services, and enterprise networks.

By adopting secure, scalable, and privacy-centric federated identity frameworks, organizations can enhance trust, streamline authentication, and protect user identities in the era of 5G.

Mobile Identity in the Metaverse

The rise of the metaverse is reshaping the digital landscape, creating immersive, interconnected virtual worlds where people interact, socialize, work, and transact. As these virtual environments expand, mobile identity will play a critical role in ensuring secure authentication, user verification, and digital trust. Unlike traditional online platforms, the metaverse requires seamless, real-time identity management across augmented reality (AR), virtual reality (VR), blockchain ecosystems, and decentralized networks. Mobile identity solutions will be essential for enabling users to navigate the metaverse securely while maintaining privacy, interoperability, and control over their digital personas.

The Role of Mobile Identity in the Metaverse

In the metaverse, users engage with virtual spaces through avatars, digital credentials, and decentralized identity frameworks. Managing these identities securely and efficiently is crucial to prevent fraud, establish trust, and enable seamless cross-platform interactions. Mobile identity serves as the foundation for authenticating users across different metaverse applications, enabling passwordless login, biometric authentication, and blockchain-based verification. By linking mobile identity to metaverse accounts, users can securely access virtual commerce, digital workplaces, gaming ecosystems, and social interactions without compromising security or convenience.

Unlike conventional online accounts that rely on centralized identity providers, the metaverse introduces decentralized identity (DID) models, where users control their own identity credentials without depending on a single authority. Mobile identity solutions, integrated with blockchain and self-sovereign identity (SSI) frameworks, enable users to authenticate themselves across different metaverse platforms while maintaining privacy and ownership over their digital identity. These decentralized identity models eliminate the need for multiple logins, enhancing security and reducing the risk of identity fraud.

Authentication and Security in the Metaverse

One of the biggest challenges in metaverse identity management is verifying user authenticity while preserving anonymity. Many users prefer to maintain pseudonymous identities in virtual environments, making it difficult to distinguish between legitimate users and malicious actors. Mobile identity solutions, powered by biometric authentication, AI-driven identity verification, and cryptographic proofs, can enable secure access without revealing sensitive personal information.

For example, zero-knowledge proofs (ZKPs) allow users to prove their identity, age, or credentials without disclosing their actual identity data. A metaverse user could verify that they are over 18 without sharing their date of birth or government-issued ID. This privacy-preserving authentication method enhances security while allowing users to maintain control over their personal data.

In addition to user authentication, device-based security plays a key role in metaverse identity management. Mobile devices serve as trusted authentication hubs, enabling secure login through one-time passcodes (OTPs), cryptographic keys, and biometric verification. Many metaverse applications will integrate multi-factor authentication (MFA) and risk-based authentication, ensuring that only legitimate users can access virtual assets and sensitive transactions.

Digital Wallets and Identity Management in the Metaverse

As the metaverse economy grows, digital wallets linked to mobile identity will become essential for managing cryptographic credentials, digital assets, and virtual currencies. Mobile identity solutions enable users to store and access their blockchain-based credentials, NFTs (non-fungible tokens), and decentralized finance (DeFi) assets securely. Instead of relying on centralized authentication providers, users can sign transactions, verify ownership of virtual properties, and authenticate digital contracts using decentralized identity wallets.

For example, a user purchasing virtual land in a metaverse environment can use their mobile identity wallet to sign a smart contract, proving ownership without exposing their real-world identity. This integration of mobile identity, digital wallets, and blockchain authentication will streamline virtual commerce, peer-to-peer transactions, and access control across different metaverse applications.

Interoperability and Cross-Platform Identity in the Metaverse

One of the major challenges in metaverse identity management is ensuring seamless authentication across multiple platforms. Currently, different virtual worlds operate independently, each requiring separate logins, identity verifications, and credentials. Mobile identity solutions, integrated with federated identity and decentralized identity (DID) frameworks, can enable cross-platform authentication, allowing users to access multiple metaverse environments using a single identity.

For example, a user could create a verified digital identity on one metaverse platform and carry it to another without re-registering. Identity federation standards such as OpenID Connect (OIDC), OAuth 2.0, and W3C's Decentralized Identifiers (DIDs) will facilitate seamless identity portability across virtual spaces, ensuring users can interact securely without friction.

Preventing Fraud and Identity Theft in the Metaverse

As the metaverse expands, identity fraud, deepfake attacks, and account takeovers will become significant security threats. Cybercriminals may attempt to impersonate users, steal virtual assets, or exploit avatar-based identity verification for malicious purposes. Mobile identity management, combined with AI-driven fraud detection, behavioral biometrics, and real-time authentication monitoring, will be essential in mitigating these risks.

For instance, AI-powered behavioral biometrics can analyze keystroke dynamics, voice recognition, and interaction patterns to detect anomalies and prevent unauthorized access. If an attacker attempts to take over a metaverse account, continuous authentication mechanisms will flag unusual behavior and require additional verification through mobile identity authentication factors.

Metaverse platforms will also need to implement real-time identity monitoring and reputation systems, allowing users to verify trust scores, past interactions, and authentication histories before engaging in transactions or social interactions. This trust-based identity model will reduce fraud while maintaining user privacy.

Regulatory and Ethical Considerations for Mobile Identity in the Metaverse

With the emergence of biometric authentication, decentralized identity, and AI-driven verification, regulatory frameworks must evolve to protect user privacy, data ownership, and consent management in the metaverse. Laws such as GDPR, CCPA, and emerging digital identity regulations will require metaverse platforms to implement privacy-preserving authentication methods, user-controlled identity management, and transparent data governance policies.

For instance, privacy-enhancing technologies (PETs) such as homomorphic encryption, differential privacy, and secure multi-party computation will enable identity verification without exposing raw identity data. Users should have the right to control, revoke, and manage their digital identities across metaverse platforms, ensuring that identity information is not misused or exploited by third parties.

The Future of Mobile Identity in the Metaverse

As metaverse ecosystems continue to evolve, mobile identity solutions will play a foundational role in securing authentication, enabling decentralized interactions, and protecting digital assets. The future of mobile identity in the metaverse will be driven by:

AI-powered identity verification to detect fraud and ensure real-time authentication.

Blockchain-based decentralized identity (DID) to give users full control over their virtual identity.

Cross-platform identity federation to enable seamless access across multiple metaverse environments.

Zero-knowledge proofs (ZKPs) for privacy-preserving authentication without exposing sensitive identity data.

Integration of biometric security with AI-driven behavioral authentication for continuous identity verification.

By leveraging mobile identity, decentralized authentication, and AI-driven security, the metaverse will become a more secure, user-centric, and privacy-preserving digital world where individuals can interact, transact, and collaborate with confidence.

Edge Computing and Identity Management

The rise of edge computing has revolutionized data processing by enabling decentralized computing closer to data sources, reducing latency, and improving real-time decision-making. As organizations shift toward edge-based architectures for IoT, cloud services, and AI-driven applications, the need for robust identity management at the edge becomes increasingly critical. Managing digital identities in edge environments presents unique challenges related to security, authentication, access control, and privacy, requiring innovative approaches to ensure seamless and secure identity verification across distributed systems.

The Role of Identity Management in Edge Computing

Edge computing processes data at local edge nodes, gateways, and devices, rather than relying on centralized cloud infrastructure. This decentralized approach enhances speed and efficiency but introduces new identity security concerns, as multiple devices, applications, and users interact across edge networks. Traditional identity and access management (IAM) models, which depend on centralized authentication servers, may not be sufficient for securing highly distributed edge environments.

In an edge computing ecosystem, identity management plays a crucial role in ensuring:

Secure device authentication: Edge nodes and IoT devices must be uniquely identifiable and authorized to interact with the network.

User and service authentication: Users accessing edge applications must verify their identity through multi-factor authentication (MFA) or biometric authentication.

Data access control: Sensitive data processed at the edge must be protected with role-based access control (RBAC) and attribute-based access control (ABAC) policies.

Zero Trust security: Edge computing requires continuous identity verification, ensuring that no device or user is trusted by default.

Decentralized Identity Management in Edge Environments

Given the distributed nature of edge computing, decentralized identity (DID) solutions are becoming a preferred approach for managing digital identities. Unlike traditional centralized identity systems that rely on cloud-based identity providers, decentralized identity allows users, devices, and applications to authenticate autonomously without a central authority.

Decentralized identity in edge computing is powered by:

Self-sovereign identity (SSI): Users and devices control their own identity credentials without relying on external identity providers.

Blockchain-based identity verification: Cryptographic authentication ensures that edge devices can verify credentials securely without requiring a central server.

Zero-knowledge proofs (ZKPs): Devices can authenticate without exposing sensitive identity data, enhancing privacy in edge transactions.

By implementing decentralized identity frameworks, organizations can reduce identity fraud, eliminate single points of failure, and enhance security across edge networks.

Authentication and Security Challenges at the Edge

Managing authentication in edge computing presents several security challenges, including:

Device Spoofing and Identity Theft: Attackers may attempt to impersonate legitimate edge devices or users to gain unauthorized access. Implementing hardware-based authentication (e.g., Trusted Platform Modules (TPM) and Secure Enclaves) can mitigate these risks.

Lack of Continuous Connectivity: Many edge devices operate in low-bandwidth environments, making real-time authentication difficult. Offline authentication models and distributed ledger-based identity verification help ensure security even in disconnected scenarios.

Data Privacy and Compliance Risks: Edge computing often processes personally identifiable information (PII) at remote locations. Organizations must implement data minimization, encryption, and compliance with GDPR, CCPA, and other privacy regulations to protect user identity data.

Scalability Issues: Managing identities across thousands (or millions) of edge nodes and IoT devices requires automated identity provisioning, certificate lifecycle management, and AI-driven access control to scale efficiently.

To overcome these challenges, organizations must adopt AI-driven security analytics, machine learning-based anomaly detection, and continuous authentication mechanisms at the edge.

Zero Trust Identity Models for Edge Security

Traditional perimeter-based security models are insufficient for edge computing, where data and applications are spread across distributed locations. The Zero Trust security model ensures that every request for access—whether from users, devices, or applications—is continuously verified before granting permissions.

A Zero Trust identity framework for edge computing includes:

Device Identity Verification: All edge devices must authenticate using cryptographic certificates, secure boot processes, and unique device IDs before connecting to the network.

Behavioral Biometrics: AI-powered identity verification analyzes keystroke patterns, device usage behavior, and contextual data to authenticate users dynamically.

Least-Privilege Access Control: Users and devices are granted the minimum necessary permissions to perform their tasks, reducing attack surfaces.

Continuous Risk-Based Authentication: Edge identity systems monitor user behavior and network activity in real time, requiring additional authentication steps if anomalies are detected.

By integrating Zero Trust identity principles, edge computing environments can enhance security while ensuring frictionless user access.

AI and Machine Learning in Edge Identity Management

Artificial intelligence (AI) and machine learning (ML) play a transformative role in identity management at the edge, enabling real-time threat detection, automated authentication, and intelligent access control.

Key AI-driven identity management applications include:

Real-Time Identity Anomaly Detection: AI-powered security analytics detect suspicious login behaviors, unauthorized device access, and insider threats at edge nodes.

Adaptive Authentication: AI continuously evaluates risk factors—such as user location, device security posture, and network trust levels—to dynamically adjust authentication requirements.

Predictive Identity Fraud Prevention: Machine learning models analyze historical attack patterns to proactively identify identity-based threats before they occur.

Intelligent Identity Orchestration: AI automates identity lifecycle management, user provisioning, and access revocation, reducing administrative overhead.

By integrating AI-driven identity security, organizations can enhance real-time identity protection while minimizing authentication friction at the edge.

Use Cases of Identity Management in Edge Computing

Smart Cities: Edge identity management enables secure authentication for connected streetlights, traffic systems, and public transportation networks, ensuring that only authorized users and devices interact with smart infrastructure.

Industrial IoT (IIoT): Factories use edge-based identity authentication to control access to automated machinery, supply chain tracking systems, and industrial robots securely.

Healthcare: Medical edge devices require biometric authentication and secure identity verification for remote patient monitoring, telemedicine, and medical device access control.

Autonomous Vehicles: Edge identity solutions allow vehicle-to-vehicle (V2V) and vehicle-to-infrastructure (V2I) authentication, ensuring safe and secure communications in connected transportation systems.

Retail and Edge AI: Retailers use edge-based facial recognition and mobile identity authentication for secure self-checkout experiences and personalized shopping.

The Future of Edge Identity Management

As edge computing adoption accelerates, identity management solutions must evolve to address new security challenges, scalability issues, and privacy concerns. Future trends in edge identity management include:

Blockchain-Based Identity for Edge Devices: Decentralized authentication models will secure IoT devices and prevent identity fraud in distributed environments.

Homomorphic Encryption and Zero-Knowledge Proofs: Privacy-enhancing technologies will enable secure identity verification without exposing sensitive data at the edge.

Quantum-Safe Identity Authentication: As quantum computing advances, organizations will adopt quantum-resistant cryptographic algorithms to future-proof edge identity security.

AI-Powered Edge Identity Threat Intelligence: Next-generation AI security platforms will detect, predict, and respond to identity threats in real time, reducing the risk of identity breaches.

By implementing scalable, AI-driven, and decentralized identity solutions, organizations can enhance security, streamline authentication, and enable seamless identity verification across the evolving edge computing landscape.

Adaptive Authentication for Mobile Users

As mobile devices become the primary gateway for digital interactions, securing user authentication while ensuring a seamless experience is more critical than ever. Traditional authentication methods, such as passwords and PINs, often fail to provide both security and convenience, leading to vulnerabilities like phishing attacks, credential stuffing, and unauthorized access. Adaptive authentication addresses these challenges by dynamically adjusting authentication requirements based on real-time risk assessments. This approach enhances security while minimizing friction for legitimate users, making it an essential component of modern identity and access management (IAM) systems.

The Concept of Adaptive Authentication

Adaptive authentication is a security framework that evaluates contextual and behavioral factors to determine the level of authentication required for a particular login attempt or transaction. Unlike static authentication methods that apply the same security measures to every login, adaptive authentication analyzes real-time risk indicators and adjusts security requirements accordingly. If a login attempt appears low-risk, the system may allow access with minimal authentication, such as biometric verification. Conversely, if a login attempt shows signs of suspicious activity, additional verification steps, such as a one-time passcode (OTP) or multi-factor authentication (MFA), may be required.

The key components of adaptive authentication include:

Context-aware authentication: Analyzing login context, including device type, geographic location, network trust level, and access history.

Risk-based authentication: Assigning a risk score to each login attempt and adjusting authentication measures dynamically.

Behavioral biometrics: Monitoring user behavior patterns, such as typing speed, screen interaction, and navigation habits, to detect anomalies.

Machine learning-based anomaly detection: Using AI to analyze authentication trends and identify deviations from normal user behavior.

By integrating these components, adaptive authentication ensures that mobile users can securely access accounts, applications, and digital services without unnecessary authentication friction.

How Adaptive Authentication Works for Mobile Users

Adaptive authentication relies on real-time data analytics to assess risk levels and determine the most appropriate authentication response. A typical adaptive authentication process follows these steps:

User Initiates Login: A user attempts to log in to a mobile app, website, or enterprise network from their smartphone or tablet.

Risk Assessment: The authentication system evaluates multiple risk indicators, including device ID, IP address, location, and previous login behavior.

Behavioral Analysis: AI-driven behavioral biometrics compare the user's typing patterns, swipe gestures, and mouse movements with past activity.

Authentication Decision: Based on the risk score, the system takes one of the following actions:

If the risk score is low, the user is granted access with minimal authentication.

If the risk score is moderate, the system may require biometric authentication (fingerprint, facial recognition).

If the risk score is high, the system may enforce multi-factor authentication (MFA) or even block access until further verification is completed.

Continuous Monitoring: Even after authentication, the system continuously monitors user behavior to detect suspicious activities and enforce session security.

This dynamic authentication process balances security and usability, allowing users to authenticate quickly while reducing the risk of fraud and unauthorized access.

Key Risk Factors Considered in Adaptive Authentication

Adaptive authentication systems analyze multiple risk signals to determine the appropriate authentication response. Some of the key factors include:

Device Trustworthiness: If the user logs in from a recognized and previously authenticated device, the authentication process may be streamlined. However, if they attempt to log in from a new or untrusted device, additional verification may be required.

Geolocation Data: If a user logs in from a familiar location, such as their home or office, authentication requirements may be relaxed. However, if an attempt is made from an unexpected country or region, a step-up authentication process may be triggered.

Time-Based Authentication Patterns: If a user typically logs in during business hours but suddenly attempts access at an unusual time, the system may flag the attempt as risky.

Network Security Level: Connections from public Wi-Fi, VPNs, or high-risk IP addresses may be treated with greater scrutiny compared to logins from secure home or corporate networks.

Login Velocity: If multiple login attempts occur within a short time from different locations, this may indicate a credential stuffing attack or unauthorized access attempt.

Behavioral Biometrics: AI-driven behavioral authentication detects subtle differences in user interactions, such as typing patterns, swiping gestures, or how the user holds their device. If deviations from normal behavior are detected, additional authentication layers may be applied.

By continuously evaluating these factors, adaptive authentication identifies and responds to threats in real time while ensuring legitimate users can authenticate effortlessly.

Benefits of Adaptive Authentication for Mobile Users

The adoption of adaptive authentication in mobile identity management provides several key advantages:

Enhanced Security: Dynamic authentication measures reduce the risk of phishing attacks, credential theft, and brute-force attacks by enforcing stronger security only when necessary.

Frictionless User Experience: Unlike traditional MFA, which requires additional steps for every login, adaptive authentication only introduces extra verification when needed, improving the overall user experience.

Fraud Prevention: AI-driven anomaly detection prevents account takeovers, mobile phishing attacks, and identity theft by blocking suspicious login attempts before they escalate.

Regulatory Compliance: Adaptive authentication helps organizations comply with data protection regulations such as GDPR, CCPA, and PSD2, which require strong authentication measures for sensitive transactions.

Seamless Integration with Mobile Identity Solutions: Adaptive authentication can be integrated with passwordless authentication, mobile identity wallets, and biometric security, ensuring a holistic security approach for mobile users.

Use Cases of Adaptive Authentication in Mobile Identity

Banking and Financial Services: Adaptive authentication ensures secure access to mobile banking apps by requiring step-up authentication for high-risk transactions, such as large fund transfers or account modifications.

E-Commerce and Digital Payments: Online retailers use adaptive authentication to protect users from fraudulent purchases, verifying identity only when an anomaly is detected.

Enterprise Security and Remote Work: Organizations enforce adaptive authentication for VPN access, cloud applications, and remote workforce security, preventing unauthorized corporate data access.

Healthcare Identity Verification: Telemedicine and health records access require adaptive authentication to protect patient data and comply with HIPAA regulations.

Social Media and Digital Platforms: Social networks and online services use adaptive authentication to detect fake accounts, prevent unauthorized logins, and reduce identity fraud.

The Future of Adaptive Authentication

As mobile identity evolves, adaptive authentication will become increasingly AI-driven, biometric-integrated, and context-aware. Future advancements will include:

AI-powered real-time risk scoring for instant fraud detection.

Blockchain-based decentralized identity to provide users with more control over authentication.

Quantum-resistant cryptographic authentication to future-proof mobile security.

5G-enhanced authentication for low-latency, real-time identity verification.

By integrating adaptive authentication with mobile identity solutions, organizations can strengthen security, improve user convenience, and build trust in digital interactions while staying ahead of emerging identity threats.

Ethical Considerations in Mobile Identity

As mobile identity management becomes increasingly integral to digital interactions, ethical considerations surrounding its implementation, use, and regulation have become a growing concern. Mobile identity solutions provide convenience, security, and efficiency, allowing users to authenticate, verify, and access services with ease. However, the way personal data is collected, stored, shared, and utilized raises serious ethical questions regarding privacy, surveillance, consent, discrimination, and digital inclusion. Ensuring that mobile identity systems are designed and implemented ethically is crucial for protecting user rights and fostering trust in digital identity ecosystems.

Privacy and User Consent

One of the most fundamental ethical concerns in mobile identity management is the protection of user privacy. Mobile identity systems collect vast amounts of personal information, including biometric data, location history, device fingerprints, and behavioral patterns. If this data is not handled responsibly, users may face unauthorized surveillance, data exploitation, and loss of control over their digital identities.

A key ethical principle in mobile identity is informed consent. Users should have clear, transparent information about what data is being collected, how it is being used, and who has access to it. Many identity verification processes require biometric authentication, such as facial recognition or fingerprint scanning, yet users often lack the ability to opt out or use alternative authentication methods. Ethical mobile

172

identity solutions must ensure that users can make informed choices about their data, with the ability to revoke consent at any time.

Organizations should adopt privacy-by-design principles, embedding strong data protection mechanisms into identity management systems. This includes data minimization (collecting only the necessary information), anonymization techniques (removing personally identifiable details), and encryption to safeguard sensitive identity data. Ensuring that users retain control over their data reinforces trust and aligns with ethical standards of digital privacy.

Surveillance and Government Use of Mobile Identity

The increasing adoption of mobile identity solutions by governments for national ID programs, digital passports, and public services raises ethical concerns about mass surveillance and civil liberties. While digital identity systems can streamline public services and improve security, they also have the potential to enable state surveillance, tracking, and the erosion of personal freedoms.

Many governments use mobile identity verification for law enforcement and national security purposes. However, without clear legal safeguards, transparency, and accountability, these systems can be misused to monitor individuals, suppress dissent, or disproportionately target marginalized communities. Ethical mobile identity frameworks must include independent oversight, strict data retention policies, and mechanisms for users to challenge unjustified surveillance.

The use of facial recognition technology (FRT) in mobile identity is particularly controversial. While it offers convenience and security, it has been linked to privacy violations, racial and gender bias, and wrongful identification. Governments and organizations must establish strict ethical guidelines governing how biometric data is collected, stored, and used, ensuring that it is not deployed for mass surveillance or discriminatory practices.

Bias and Discrimination in Mobile Identity Systems

Machine learning and artificial intelligence (AI) are increasingly used in mobile identity verification, from biometric recognition to fraud detection and risk-based authentication. However, AI-driven identity systems have been shown to exhibit biases based on race, gender, age, and socioeconomic status, leading to discrimination in access to services.

For example, studies have shown that facial recognition algorithms have higher error rates for darker skin tones, resulting in misidentifications and access denials for certain demographic groups. If mobile identity systems are not trained on diverse datasets, they risk reinforcing discrimination and inequality. Organizations developing mobile identity solutions must prioritize algorithmic fairness, continuous bias testing, and diverse data representation to prevent discriminatory outcomes.

In financial services, risk-based authentication models may use AI to determine the likelihood of fraud, leading to unfair profiling based on behavioral patterns, location data, or device usage. Ethical mobile identity frameworks must ensure that automated decision-making processes are transparent, explainable, and challengeable, preventing algorithmic bias from disproportionately affecting vulnerable populations.

Digital Inclusion and Accessibility

Mobile identity solutions should be designed to promote inclusion rather than create barriers. However, digital identity systems often exclude individuals who lack smartphones, reliable internet access, or digital literacy skills. Vulnerable groups, such as elderly individuals, low-income populations, refugees, and people with disabilities, may struggle to use mobile identity systems, limiting their access to essential services.

Ethical mobile identity initiatives should prioritize digital accessibility, ensuring that authentication methods accommodate diverse user needs. This includes:

Providing alternative authentication options (e.g., PINs, voice recognition, physical ID verification) for users without smartphones.

Designing user-friendly interfaces with clear instructions and support for multiple languages.

Ensuring compliance with accessibility standards, such as Web Content Accessibility Guidelines (WCAG), for individuals with disabilities.

Digital identity should be a tool for empowerment, not exclusion. Governments and organizations must work to bridge the digital divide, ensuring that mobile identity services are affordable, accessible, and usable by all.

Data Ownership and Decentralized Identity Models

A central ethical question in mobile identity management is who owns user identity data. Many digital identity systems are managed by corporations, governments, or third-party identity providers, raising concerns about data monopolization, exploitation, and breaches.

The emergence of decentralized identity (DID) and self-sovereign identity (SSI) frameworks offers an ethical alternative. These models return control of digital identity to individuals, allowing them to manage and verify their credentials without reliance on central authorities. Using blockchain-based verifiable credentials, users can authenticate themselves securely while maintaining privacy and autonomy.

Decentralized identity solutions align with ethical principles by:

Eliminating unnecessary data collection (users disclose only the information required for a specific transaction).

Reducing reliance on centralized databases, which are prime targets for breaches.

Giving users full control over identity sharing and revocation.

However, decentralized identity also raises ethical concerns regarding adoption, governance, and trust. Organizations must ensure that DID solutions are interoperable, user-friendly, and legally recognized, preventing fragmentation and accessibility issues.

Regulatory and Ethical Frameworks for Mobile Identity

To uphold ethical standards in mobile identity management, organizations and governments must comply with global data protection regulations, including:

General Data Protection Regulation (GDPR) – Ensuring user consent, data minimization, and the right to be forgotten.

California Consumer Privacy Act (CCPA) – Giving users greater control over their personal data.

Biometric Information Privacy Act (BIPA) – Regulating biometric data collection and requiring explicit user consent.

Ethical mobile identity frameworks should go beyond legal compliance by embedding fairness, transparency, and accountability into identity management systems. This includes:

Establishing ethical review boards to oversee mobile identity deployments.

Providing clear recourse mechanisms for users to challenge identity-related decisions.

Engaging stakeholders, including privacy advocates, technologists, and civil rights groups, in identity policy discussions.

Building an Ethical Future for Mobile Identity

The future of mobile identity must balance security, convenience, and human rights, ensuring that identity systems are equitable, privacy-preserving, and inclusive. By prioritizing user control, minimizing data collection, and mitigating bias, organizations can build ethical mobile identity solutions that enhance trust and protect individuals in the digital age.

Challenges and Opportunities in Mobile Identity

Mobile identity has emerged as a cornerstone of digital security, enabling users to authenticate themselves, access services, and conduct transactions from their smartphones and other connected devices. As organizations and governments continue to implement mobile identity solutions, they encounter both significant challenges and transformative opportunities. Balancing security, privacy, user experience, and regulatory compliance is essential for building robust mobile identity systems that are both secure and accessible.

Challenges in Mobile Identity

Security Threats and Identity Fraud

One of the most pressing challenges in mobile identity management is the increasing sophistication of cyber threats. Mobile identity systems are prime targets for phishing attacks, credential theft, and account takeovers. Attackers use methods such as SIM swapping, man-in-the-middle (MitM) attacks, and social engineering to gain unauthorized access to user accounts.

Biometric authentication, such as facial recognition and fingerprint scanning, has improved security, but it is not immune to spoofing and deepfake attacks. Criminals are developing advanced techniques to bypass biometric authentication using AI-generated synthetic identities. Organizations must continuously update their security frameworks to include liveness detection, anti-spoofing measures, and behavioral biometrics to counter these evolving threats.

Balancing Security and User Experience

Mobile identity solutions must provide strong authentication while maintaining a seamless user experience. Traditional security measures, such as passwords and multi-factor authentication (MFA), often introduce friction in the login process, leading to user frustration and abandonment.

Adaptive authentication, which dynamically adjusts security requirements based on risk levels, has emerged as a solution. However, implementing it effectively without overwhelming users with frequent authentication prompts remains a challenge. Organizations must strike the right balance between security and convenience, ensuring that authentication processes remain frictionless yet resilient against cyber threats.

Interoperability Across Platforms and Services

The mobile identity landscape is fragmented, with different platforms, applications, and service providers using varying authentication standards. This lack of interoperability complicates cross-platform authentication and limits seamless user experiences.

Federated identity solutions, such as OAuth 2.0, OpenID Connect (OIDC), and Security Assertion Markup Language (SAML), have helped address this challenge, but many services still operate in isolated ecosystems. Users often juggle multiple identity credentials across platforms, leading to security risks such as password reuse and identity duplication.

The emergence of decentralized identity (DID) and self-sovereign identity (SSI) offers a potential solution by allowing users to manage their identities independently across different services. However, widespread adoption of these models requires collaboration between governments, enterprises, and standards organizations to create unified identity frameworks.

Regulatory and Compliance Complexities

Mobile identity management must comply with global data protection and privacy regulations, such as GDPR (General Data Protection Regulation), CCPA (California Consumer Privacy Act), and eIDAS (Electronic Identification, Authentication, and Trust Services). These regulations require organizations to:

Obtain user consent before collecting identity data.

Implement data minimization to collect only necessary information.

Ensure secure storage and encryption of personal identity data.

Provide users with control over their data through access, modification, and deletion rights.

Navigating these compliance requirements is challenging, especially for global enterprises operating across multiple jurisdictions. Organizations must adopt privacy-by-design principles, ensuring that mobile identity solutions adhere to regulatory frameworks while remaining flexible for future changes in legislation.

Digital Inclusion and Accessibility

Mobile identity should be accessible to all users, but digital exclusion remains a significant challenge. Individuals without smartphones, stable internet connections, or digital literacy skills often struggle to access digital identity systems, creating barriers to essential services such as banking, healthcare, and government benefits.

Ethical mobile identity solutions should prioritize inclusive authentication methods, such as:

Alternative verification options for users without biometric-compatible devices.

Voice-based authentication for individuals with visual impairments.

Offline authentication solutions for users in low-connectivity regions.

Governments and organizations must invest in digital literacy programs and affordable identity solutions to ensure that mobile identity does not widen the digital divide.

Opportunities in Mobile Identity

Passwordless Authentication and Biometric Advancements

One of the most promising advancements in mobile identity is the move towards passwordless authentication. Traditional passwords are prone to security vulnerabilities, and users often struggle with password fatigue and reuse.

Passwordless authentication methods, including biometric authentication, cryptographic keys, and mobile push notifications, enhance security while improving user experience. Solutions such as FIDO2 authentication and passkeys eliminate the need for passwords altogether, reducing the risk of phishing and credential theft.

The integration of multi-modal biometrics, such as combining facial recognition with voice authentication or behavioral biometrics, further enhances security and usability. AI-driven liveness detection ensures that biometric authentication cannot be bypassed using spoofing techniques.

Blockchain-Based Decentralized Identity

Decentralized identity (DID) and self-sovereign identity (SSI) present a transformative shift in mobile identity management. Instead of relying on centralized identity providers (such as governments, social media platforms, or corporations), decentralized identity solutions use blockchain-based verifiable credentials to give users full control over their identity data.

Benefits of decentralized identity include:

Improved privacy – Users can authenticate themselves without revealing unnecessary personal information.

Reduced identity fraud – Blockchain's immutability prevents identity tampering.

Interoperability – Decentralized identity can be used across multiple platforms without reliance on a single provider.

Governments, financial institutions, and enterprises are increasingly exploring DID solutions for digital IDs, travel credentials, and financial transactions, paving the way for a more secure and user-controlled identity ecosystem.

AI and Machine Learning for Identity Fraud Prevention

Artificial intelligence (AI) and machine learning (ML) are revolutionizing mobile identity security by enabling real-time fraud detection, behavioral analytics, and anomaly detection. AI-driven identity verification can:

Analyze login patterns and user behavior to detect anomalies.

Prevent synthetic identity fraud by identifying inconsistencies in identity data.

Enhance continuous authentication by monitoring real-time device interactions.

AI-powered identity solutions reduce reliance on static credentials and enable dynamic risk-based authentication, ensuring that security measures adapt to emerging threats.

5G and Edge Computing Enhancing Mobile Identity

The rollout of 5G networks and edge computing presents new opportunities for low-latency, real-time authentication. 5G enables:

Faster biometric authentication for seamless mobile identity verification.

Edge-based identity processing to reduce dependency on cloud authentication.

Enhanced security for IoT devices by enabling real-time identity verification at the edge.

5G-driven mobile identity solutions will power smart cities, autonomous vehicles, and next-generation IoT applications, making secure identity management an integral part of digital transformation.

The Future of Mobile Identity

As mobile identity continues to evolve, the industry must overcome security challenges, enhance interoperability, and promote ethical digital inclusion. By leveraging passwordless authentication, decentralized identity, AI-driven fraud detection, and 5G advancements, mobile identity solutions will become more secure, user-friendly, and accessible. Organizations that embrace innovation while addressing privacy concerns and regulatory compliance will play a key role in shaping the future of secure digital identity ecosystems.

Conclusion and Future Research Directions

Mobile identity management has emerged as a fundamental pillar of digital security, transforming how individuals authenticate, access services, and safeguard their personal data. The evolution of biometric authentication, decentralized identity, adaptive authentication, and AI-driven fraud detection has significantly enhanced the security and usability of mobile identity solutions. However, as mobile identity continues to evolve, several challenges remain, including privacy concerns, security threats, interoperability issues, regulatory compliance, and digital inclusion. Addressing these challenges requires continued research, technological advancements, and collaborative efforts between governments, enterprises, and technology providers.

Key Takeaways from Mobile Identity Research

The development of mobile identity management has revealed several critical insights that define the current state and future trajectory of digital identity security:

Security and Privacy Balance – While passwordless authentication, biometric verification, and AI-powered fraud prevention have strengthened mobile identity security, privacy concerns surrounding biometric data storage, data sharing, and surveillance risks remain significant. Research must focus on privacy-enhancing technologies (PETs), such as homomorphic encryption, zero-knowledge proofs (ZKPs), and differential privacy, to ensure strong authentication while protecting user privacy.

Decentralized and Self-Sovereign Identity (SSI) – Traditional identity systems rely on centralized identity providers, increasing the risk of data breaches, identity theft, and government overreach. Decentralized identity models, based on blockchain and verifiable credentials, offer a promising alternative by giving users greater control over their digital identities. However, scalability, interoperability, and regulatory challenges must be addressed before SSI becomes mainstream.

Artificial Intelligence in Identity Management – AI and machine learning have revolutionized fraud detection, risk-based authentication, and continuous identity verification. However, concerns about bias in AI-driven identity systems, explainability of AI decisions, and ethical concerns in automated identity verification require further research. Developing transparent and fair AI models is essential to prevent discrimination and exclusion in mobile identity authentication.

Regulatory and Compliance Challenges – Compliance with GDPR, CCPA, eIDAS, PSD2, and biometric privacy laws (such as BIPA) requires businesses to implement strict data protection, user consent mechanisms, and security best practices. As mobile identity continues to evolve, governments must establish global identity standards and frameworks to ensure consistent privacy, security, and ethical identity management across borders.

The Role of 5G, IoT, and Edge Computing in Identity Management – The rise of 5G networks, edge computing, and the Internet of Things (IoT) has introduced new identity management challenges. Traditional authentication models may not be sufficient for securing millions of connected devices that require real-time identity verification and decentralized access control. Future identity management solutions must leverage AI-driven identity orchestration, Zero Trust security, and federated authentication frameworks to secure the next generation of digital ecosystems.

Future Research Directions in Mobile Identity

While significant progress has been made in mobile identity management, several research areas require further exploration to enhance security, privacy, usability, and accessibility. The following key research directions will shape the future of mobile identity:

1. Privacy-Preserving Authentication and Data Minimization

Future research should focus on privacy-enhancing identity verification methods that allow users to prove their identity without exposing unnecessary personal data. Technologies such as:

Zero-knowledge proofs (ZKPs) – Enable users to verify attributes (e.g., proving they are over 18) without revealing their full identity.

Anonymous credentials and selective disclosure – Allow users to share only the required information without exposing additional sensitive details.

Federated learning and privacy-preserving AI – Develop machine learning models that process identity data without centralizing personal information.

Ensuring strong authentication while reducing data exposure will enhance user privacy and trust in mobile identity systems.

2. Decentralized Identity Interoperability and Standardization

While self-sovereign identity (SSI) and decentralized identity (DID) provide greater user control, lack of standardization and interoperability remains a challenge. Research should explore:

Cross-platform decentralized identity frameworks that integrate blockchain, verifiable credentials, and decentralized identifiers (DIDs) across multiple ecosystems.

Global regulatory models for decentralized identity adoption, ensuring legal recognition and compliance with existing privacy laws.

Scalable decentralized authentication protocols that can support millions of transactions per second without compromising security.

Developing interoperable decentralized identity solutions will enable seamless authentication across different industries and jurisdictions.

3. AI-Driven Continuous Authentication and Behavioral Biometrics

AI-powered continuous authentication is an emerging field that enhances security by analyzing real-time user behavior. Future research should focus on:

Multi-modal biometric authentication, combining fingerprint, facial recognition, voice, and gait analysis for stronger authentication.

Adaptive AI-driven risk-based authentication, dynamically adjusting security requirements based on user behavior and device context.

Behavioral biometrics and anomaly detection, identifying identity fraud based on keystroke dynamics, touchscreen interactions, and mouse movement patterns.

Improving AI-based authentication models will provide strong security without disrupting user experience.

4. Secure Mobile Identity for IoT and Smart Devices

With the rapid growth of smart cities, autonomous vehicles, and industrial IoT, securing device identity and authentication is a top research priority. Future developments should include:

Lightweight identity authentication for resource-constrained IoT devices, enabling secure identity management with minimal processing power.

Blockchain-based IoT identity verification, ensuring device authenticity without relying on centralized authorities.

Edge computing identity security, providing real-time authentication at the edge to reduce latency and improve security for critical IoT applications.

These advancements will enable secure, scalable mobile identity frameworks for IoT environments.

5. Ethical and Legal Considerations in Biometric Identity Management

The use of biometric authentication raises significant ethical concerns related to privacy, consent, and bias. Future research should address:

Ethical guidelines for biometric data collection and storage, ensuring transparency and user control over biometric identifiers.

Bias reduction in AI-based identity verification, preventing discrimination against certain demographic groups.

Regulatory frameworks for biometric identity governance, ensuring compliance with privacy laws such as GDPR, BIPA, and CCPA.

By developing fair, transparent, and privacy-preserving biometric authentication methods, researchers can strengthen user trust and mitigate ethical risks.

Final Thoughts on the Future of Mobile Identity

The field of mobile identity management is evolving rapidly, driven by technological advancements in biometrics, AI, blockchain, and adaptive authentication. While significant progress has been made, security challenges, privacy concerns, and ethical dilemmas remain unresolved. Future research must focus on enhancing privacy, reducing authentication friction, ensuring regulatory compliance, and improving interoperability to create secure, user-centric mobile identity ecosystems.

The successful adoption of mobile identity solutions will depend on global collaboration between governments, businesses, and technology innovators. By embracing privacy-first principles, AI-driven fraud prevention, decentralized identity models, and adaptive authentication, the future of mobile identity will be more secure, inclusive, and resilient against emerging digital threats.